Know yourself. Be true to yourself. Assist and inspire where you can, and take with a grain of salt anybody who wants to pull you into a ruckus of mindless noise and distraction.

ASTROLOGY OFFERS US THE TOOLS TO WORK WITH IN-STREAMING COSMIC FORCES IN A CONSCIOUS WAY

First, we learn to understand our own unique energetic patterns.
Then we tune in and listen to what is in-streaming.
Now we can aim for collaboration with the 'Great All that Is'
as we shape our lives.

WE HAVE ALL COME TO EARTH WITH A MISSION

We may share a direction, but we each carry unique capacities and impulses that are wholly individual. When we're in alignment with the cosmic forces, the memory of our pre-earthly mission becomes clearer. We feel it in our bones as a sacred knowing. Where we lacked confidence, we can now experience a grounded certainty in how we move through, interact and transform our lives and the greater World. Let's start exploring some of the ways that you may choose to use this Astrology Diary.

Some common questions and thoughts on how to use this diary

ARE THE MONTHS THE SAME?

We've divided this Diary into '12 seasons'.
The Sun's movement through the Zodiac dictates each one.
Months are the same, as are all the dates.

WHY FOLLOW THE SUN, MOON, MERCURY, VENUS & MARS THROUGH THE ZODIAC?

Each Planet has its own personality and is influenced
by each Constellation with particular nuances and character.

- A journey around the Zodiac is a voyage through twelve
distinct viewpoints.
- In this Diary we explore these twelve points of view expressed through
the personalities of the Sun, Moon, Mercury, Venus and Mars and how we
may detect their influences in our daily lives.

WHAT IS EXPERIENTIAL ASTROLOGY?

Learning is most potent
when we come to understanding through experience.

- As each planet enters a new Zodiac Sign, you will be introduced to them.
I have used imaginative imagery to convey aspects of their personality.
They might sound like someone you know, or you may recognise
an aspect of yourself.

- There is space for journaling your experience with meeting these energies. Sometimes it might be crystal clear – other times just a vague feeling. Just jot it down without judgement. This is a deep spiritual practice, you have your whole life to unfold you – allow time and space for realisations to emerge. It gets really interesting once you start to recognise patterns... and you will!
- Sharing this journey with like-minded friends who can speak the language, or are looking to learn, can amp it up a notch. Nothing like sharing insights and experiences and having a good laugh – or cry with someone who really GETS it.
- Note down dreams, feelings, conversations, and synchronicities or simply stream your feelings out.
- This Diary will become your own Astrological logbook of soul experiences.

WHY SO MUCH ABOUT THE MOON?

It takes a year for the Sun to complete a circuit whereas the Moon flies around the Zodiac every month and is so close we can watch her journey through the night sky.

- The Moon influences, augments and highlights whichever planet she interacts with.
- There is ample space for Intention Setting and Full Moon reflections as well as space for amendments and insights on the First and Third Quarter Moons.
- Exact times are given; you can tune in then or on the surrounding days. We all experience the timing differently. Some on the day before, some the day after. Can you detect your pattern?

The Moon Cycles

THE NEW MOON
PLANTING SEEDS

The night sky is at its darkest. We can picture her like a seed in the belly of the Earth, carrying all former cycles within, yet preparing to begin again. Now is the time to set intentions for the month ahead, to prepare for new projects and let go of what we have outgrown.

1st QUARTER MOON
MOMENTUM & GROWTH

The little seed has pushed through the soil, forming a shoot and branching out with the first offering of leaves. Our course is set, and we start to see which direction our project/intentions are going. Time to make decisions, face where we are and make shifts and amendments to stay on course.

FULL MOON

PEAK ENERGY,
BLESSINGS & BLOSSOMS

Branches have fanned out and, atop the canopy of lush leaves, buds have opened into blossoms, bearing the promise of sweet fruit. The Moon is fully illumined and in her most powerful phase. We can let go of the growth period, celebrate and appreciate our achievements thus far. A time of heightened intuition and sensitivity.

3rd QUARTER MOON

REFLECT & RELEASE

Blossoms give way to ripened fruit, some harvested and some left for the earth, returning to the soil. Halfway between the Full and the next New Moon, Her energy begins to fade. Now is the time to release and forgive, reconnect and realign with our receptive, quiet, self. The fruit melts away revealing the Seed, which prepares to carry the next cycle forwards. A time of quiet and rest.

ECLIPSE SEASON
AND THE DOOR BETWEEN WORLDS

Eclipses occur on the New and the Full Moon and during these potent and potentially mythic times we take a break from working with the intention/manifestation cycle.

In the Week leading up to the Lunar Eclipse you may begin to feel that the balance is a little off; you may catch a whiff of mania on the wind. That something slightly hectic and frenetic in the air feeling is letting you know that a date has been set and the guests are beginning their own preparations for the event.

On the Lunar Eclipse, a door between worlds yawns open. What streams through is impossible to predict – it's created by an absence of light. It isn't something to be afraid of, but it is something to be respected. This is why a growing number of voices hazard caution around holding rituals on Eclipses; it's a powerful and chaotic time.

With the Solar Eclipse, on the New Moon, two weeks later the portal closes. Having supped in the worlds of the Humans, the visitors say their goodbyes, trailing their splintered stars and banners shredded from the stuff of blackholes.

By all means, if you prefer to set intentions, do so. For those who don't, you'll find I have left room for observations. Note who, or what streamed through the portal to greet you. And also whom, or what, got sucked into another dimension, far from the regular pattern of your daily life.

WHAT ARE TRANSITS?

As the Planets move through the Signs they form connections to one another. These are called aspects; each aspect indicates the tone of communication. Some are helpful, some pushy, some intimate, and others confrontational.

WILL THEY AFFECT EVERYBODY THE SAME WAY?

No. Your Birth Chart is a capture of the Heavens the moment you were born. The Planets are spread across your chart in a unique way. They connect with each travelling Planet accordingly.
- You will find a selection of transits throughout the year, a type of 'Astro weather report'. Some may resonate, others may skip you but reach a friend.

WHY IS THERE SO MUCH GOING ON SOMETIMES AND THEN NOTHING?

Each Planet travels in their own sweet time. Sometimes they all gather in a sign. Like us at a party, in a particular city, on a certain day. Other times they go it alone, except Mercury and Venus, who never stray too far from the Sun.

I have exhausted all the questions I can think of!
It is my sincere prayer that the Astro Diary is a force for good in your life.
May it enrich your contemplations as your life unfolds.
Have a wonderful year!

Ariel Korobacz

Thank you for travelling with us

REACH OUT AND CONNECT

Everytime I get a notification that one of you Magical Souls has shared an Astro Diary post, I experience a smile that begins at my toes. Want to give an Astrologer/Artist/Writer a little joy?

Tag us over on instagram @_astro_diary_

You can email pics and feedback via 'contact us' on our website

astro-diary.com

If you are a post internet wilderness hermit, send a letter!

22 Church street - Geeveston - Tasmania - Australia 7116

ASTROLOGY READINGS

Interested in exploring your Personal Birth Chart?

Bring ALL your questions about ANY area of your life, such as:

Work, children, relationships, money and family dynamics.

Visit our website to learn more and to book your session.

astro-diary.com

Wishing you courage and love as you make your way in this big, wide world.

Ariel Korobacz

Woven Threads

Under and over our lives interweave,
Our stories the threads of a shared tapestry.

The light and the shade and the patterns we leave,
The love we share and the pain we grieve.

The currents which pull and give life to the stream,
The choices that lead to our own suffering.

The gifts we give and those we receive
The journey that opens our hearts to believe.

High Stars guide our way
Through the dark and back to day,
These shining threads of destiny
Weave us through life's tapestry.

A song of destiny by Belinda Kelly

SUN IN CAPRICORN
Surveying the Kingdom

THE TENTH HOUSE - CARDINAL EARTH
PLANETARY RULER - SATURN

Toronto 21st December - 20th January
London, Sydney 22nd December - 20th January

Picture a clock face. Now picture the Sun entering Capricorn at midnight
– at the zenith of the astrological cycle. Just like a mountain goat that has
scaled the most improbable peak, we stand at the cusp of the new year.
We can see where we've come from and the road ahead.
There is silence at these heights.

Pause just a moment though. There is still more than a week until the
New Year begins so it may not be time just yet for us to reach the quiet,
breathe out and reflect on the essence of the year. We may still be
consumed by final work deadlines and festivities that need organising,
and worried about fretful upcoming family combinations and blown out
budgets. These can threaten our sure footing and sometimes our sanity.

But that storm passes and the Sun marches proudly through the
Capricorn heavens... leading us to holidays and a pause from our
regular routines and habits. Here, in between the 9-to-5 of our lives
we can find moments of quiet and reflection. The past, the present
and the future, swirling together in a moment of clarity.

Look how far you've come... at what you have accomplished so far
and imagine the wonders you can achieve in the year ahead!

The Capricorn Sun empowers us to pragmatically plan the year ahead. He
knows what we need to achieve our goals. Tune in and listen. He is speaking
directly to you – and is quite possibly the most effective life coach ever!

Capricorn season
CONSIDERATIONS

What have you achieved over the past year?
What remains undone – what responsibilities
need to be carried into the New Year?
Where do you want to be by the end of next year?
What's your plan and how will you achieve it?
(Breaking it down into incremental steps may be helpful)

THURSDAY
21st DECEMBER

morning

afternoon

SUN ENTERS CAPRICORN
Toronto - 10.27pm

MOON ENTERS TAURUS
Toronto - 9.50pm

FRIDAY
22nd DECEMBER

morning

afternoon

SUN ENTERS CAPRICORN
London - 3.27am, Sydney - 2.27pm

MOON ENTERS TAURUS
London - 2.50am, Sydney - 1.50pm

SATURDAY
23rd DECEMBER

morning

afternoon

SUNDAY
24th DECEMBER

morning

afternoon

MOON ENTERS
GEMINI
Toronto - 3.16am, London - 8.16am,
Sydney - 7.16pm

FULL MOON
Cancer

PEAK ENERGY,
BLESSINGS & BLOSSOMS

26th December - Toronto 7.34pm
27th December - London 12.34am,
Sydney 11.34am

The mother of all Full Moons illuminates the night sky. The Sun shines from the gloriously structured halls of Capricorn. The riches of Jupiter in Taurus, combined with the mature wisdom of Saturn in Pisces support her. This is the feminine, held and supported by the masculine principle. She is the mother supported in the holy task of nurturing, raising and educating the next generation. We are all part of the complex chain of generations, whether we have children or not. We can share our care and knowledge with the children in our circle. If we find ourselves alone, the conditions are perfect for our inner child to emerge and be cherished.

MY EXPERIENCE OF THIS FULL MOON ...

VENUS

IN *Sagittarius*

Toronto, London 29th December - 23rd January
Sydney 30th December - 23rd January

THE MUSE

Venus works in the sphere of love, desire, creativity and relationships. She influences our personal magnetism, tastes and resources.

LOVE AND DESIRE

She yearns for idealism AND honesty in love, preferring independence and solitude to anything stifling or milquetoast. She inspires BIG love, the kind that makes you burn with the potential of it – that makes you feel the adventure of it.

CREATIVITY AND INSPIRATION

The Sagittarian face of the Muse will lead you down unknown pathways, beyond your comfort zone into thoughts, places and feelings that you haven't met before. Take her hand – go with it. Embrace the expansion of your inner world. Be inspired by what and whom you encounter.

THE MANNER OF RELATING

She inspires the solo traveler, but also the meeting of individuals and their tribe. Think bonding through shared ideals, goals and musical tastes. You know them when you meet them. They know you as well.

When Venus is in Sagittarius you may experience: Warm, generous, creative, and vivacious moods and encounters. Loyalty, spontaneity, and enthusiasm.

Loyal - Fickle
Warm and Generous - Careless and Absent
Spontaneous and Enthusiastic - Frivolous without Consequence

The week ahead

M

_____

T

_____

W

_____

T

_____

F

_____

S

_____

S

_____

The weekly transits

Full Moon in Cancer
Venus in Sagittarius
Mercury Stations in Sagittarius

morning

_____

afternoon

_____

TUESDAY
26th DECEMBER

morning

afternoon

WEDNESDAY
27th DECEMBER

morning

afternoon

THURSDAY
28th DECEMBER

morning

Pencil
Headache
Cleaned dog room

afternoon

Sterilized

FRIDAY
29th DECEMBER

morning

afternoon

MOON ENTERS LEO
London - 12.23am, Sydney - 11.23am

VENUS ENTERS SAGITTARIUS
Toronto - 5.24pm, London - 10.24pm

MOON ENTERS LEO
Toronto - 7.23pm

SATURDAY
30th DECEMBER

morning

afternoon

**VENUS ENTERS
SAGITTARIUS**
Sydney - 7.24am

**MERCURY STATIONS
IN SAGITTARIUS**

SUNDAY
31st DECEMBER

morning

afternoon

MOON ENTERS VIRGO
Toronto - 6.54am, London - 11.54am,
Sydney - 10.54pm

Transits

SUN IN CAPRICORN
SQUARE CHIRON IN ARIES

1st through 11th January
Heightened Influence 5th through 7th January

When Capricorn is activated, pragmatism and practicality step up to rule. Mind over matter. It's powerful. But just check, what happens if you keep pushing ever onwards and suddenly find that you're running on empty? Take time to refill. That said, sometimes we get stretched, and it can be wise to take care of what's come up before it grows and requires a far more complex and urgent remedy.

3rd QUARTER MOON

Libra

REFLECT & RELEASE

3rd January Toronto - 10.30pm
4th January London - 3.30am Sydney 2.30pm

There is a lot to process after the holiday season.
Packing, cleaning up and farewelling family. Getting used to saying 2024.
As the Moon ebbs in Libra, follow her gentle prompts
to untangle any threads that have knotted, but be gentle on yourself.
Remember it's important to take time to rest and process.
Time spent with family is a gift, but it can, at times, also be confronting.

WHAT HAVE I ACHIEVED
AND WHAT DO I NEED TO RELEASE?

MARS

IN *Capricorn*

Toronto, London 4th January - 14th February
Sydney 5th January - 15th February

THE WARRIOR

Mars works through our drives and desires; our ambitions and how we achieve them. He sets and secures our personal boundaries and defends us against those who transgress them.

DRIVES AND DESIRES

Mars in Capricorn is driven to create a lasting legacy. This is Mars coloured by Saturn, think: dignity, reputation and maturity as in finely aged (like whisky, wine or oak).

AMBITION AND WORK

Driven, but never hasty, he is consistent and self motivated. He inspires well-thought-through plans and impeccable craftsmanship.

BOUNDARIES AND PROTECTION

Mars in Capricorn can see a loose boundary wobble and lunge towards offenders before the first transgression into his personal space, and, you've picked it, this won't be tolerated. He is highly efficient at removing unwanted distractions from his personal, and familial, orbits.

When Mars is in Capricorn you may experience: Physical endurance, a strong will, a heightened capacity for self-motivation and self-reliance.

Difficulties you may encounter: Self-doubt, workaholism, isolationism, blind ambition and a need to control the world around you.

INTENTIONS, INSIGHTS AND ACCOMPLISHMENTS

The week ahead

M

T

W

T

F

S

S

The weekly transits

Mercury Stations direct in Sagittarius
Third Quarter Moon in Libra
Sun in Capricorn square Chiron in Aries
Mars enters Capricorn

morning

afternoon

MERCURY STATIONS DIRECT IN SAGITTARIUS

Toronto - 10.08 pm

TUESDAY
2nd JANUARY

morning

afternoon

MERCURY STATIONS DIRECT IN SAGITTARIUS

London - 3.08 am, Sydney - 2.08pm

WEDNESDAY
3rd JANUARY

morning

Tarot reading.
- Money
- Balance - February
- Sucess + motion until April
Rebirth - May

afternoon

Partnership - June
- Letting go + fear
- Balance

December - support from husband.

3rd QUARTER MOON IN Libra

Toronto - 10.30am

THURSDAY
4th JANUARY

morning

afternoon

3rd QUARTER MOON
IN *Libra*
London - 3.30am, Sydney - 2.30pm

MARS ENTERS
CAPRICORN
Toronto - 9.58am, London - 2.58pm

FRIDAY
5th JANUARY

morning

afternoon

MARS ENTERS
CAPRICORN
Sydney - 1.58am

SUN IN CAPRICORN
SQUARE CHIRON IN
ARIES.
Heightened Influence today
through to 7th January

SATURDAY
6th JANUARY

morning

afternoon

SUNDAY
7th JANUARY

morning

afternoon

MOON ENTERS
SAGITTARIUS
Toronto - 4.09pm, London - 9.09pm

NEW MOON

Capricorn

PLANTING SEEDS

11th January - Toronto 6.57am,
London 11.57am, Sydney 10.57pm

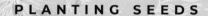

Motivation is such a mysterious thing, some people seem to know how to access it, while others languish and wait for an external prod. This New Moon is a great time to reflect on what motivates you to achieve your goals. Also, because there's always a flip side, what holds you back from taking your place in the external world? Think career, business, governance, and politics (of all sizes). There's a hefty dose of ambition in the air, consider how you might be able to utilise it.

New Moon in Capricorn themes: Unfolding your gifts into the world, ambition, pacing yourself for success. Strength, emotional endurance and character.

NEW MOON INTENTIONS

....

....

....

....

....

Transits

SUN IN CAPRICORN
TRINE URANUS IN TAURUS

5th through 15th January
Heightened Influence 9th through 11th January

Make room for the unexpected! You never, ever know what form Uranus will show up in, but as he makes a harmonious aspect with the Sun, anticipate high spirits, energy and spontaneity. Keep in mind, whatever shakes loose doesn't need to settle back in place; enjoy the gift of a gentle change.

SUN IN CAPRICORN
SQUARE THE NORTH NODE IN ARIES

10th through 16th January
Heightened Influence 10th through 12th January

It can be frustrating when we don't meet our goals, and it feels like we're slipping backwards. Don't give up, keep to the plan. This is a moment of growth, keep applying the pressure.

The week ahead

M

T

W

T

F

S

S

The weekly transits

New Moon in Capricorn
Sun in Capricorn trine Uranus in Taurus
Sun in Capricorn square the North
Node in Aries

morning

afternoon

**MOON ENTERS
SAGITTARIUS**
Toronto - 4.09pm, London - 9.09pm

TUESDAY
9th JANUARY

morning

afternoon

MOON ENTERS SAGITTARIUS
Sydney - 8.09am

MOON ENTERS CAPRICORN
Toronto - 8.34pm

SUN IN CAPRICORN TRINE URANUS IN TAURUS
Heightened Influence today through to 11th January

WEDNESDAY
10th JANUARY

morning

afternoon

MOON ENTERS CAPRICORN
London - 1.34am, Sydney - 12.34pm

SUN IN CAPRICORN SQUARE THE NORTH NODE IN ARIES
Heightened Influence today through to 12th January

THURSDAY
11th JANUARY

morning

afternoon

NEW MOON IN
Capricorn
Toronto - 6.57am, London - 11.57am,
Sydney - 10.57pm

**MOON ENTERS
AQUARIUS**
Toronto - 10.02pm

FRIDAY
12th JANUARY

morning

afternoon

**MOON ENTERS
AQUARIUS**
London - 3.02am, Sydney - 2.02pm

SATURDAY
13th JANUARY

morning

afternoon

MOON ENTERS PISCES
Toronto - 10.29pm

MERCURY RE-ENTERS CAPRICORN
Toronto - 9.50pm

SUNDAY
14th JANUARY

morning

Yoga class #2

afternoon

MOON ENTERS PISCES
London - 3.29am, Sydney - 2.29pm

MERCURY RE-ENTERS CAPRICORN
London - 2.50am, Sydney - 1.50pm

1st QUARTER MOON

Aries

MOMENTUM & GROWTH

17th January - Toronto 10.52pm
18th January - London 3.52am, Sydney 2.52pm

Grab hold of the Aries impulse to push through whatever blockages you are facing. Venus is adding her influence from fiery Sagittarius. This impulse you're feeling – is it in alignment with your highest goals? If so, go for it! We can use the assistance of fire to get, and stay, motivated. Neptune is beaming-in his mysterious influence, so stay tuned for inspiration coming from the most intangible of sources.

WHAT ACTIONS AM I TAKING TO FULFIL INTENTIONS SET ON THE NEW MOON?

....

....

....

....

....

....

PLUTO
IN *Aquarius*

from 2023 - 2044

IT'S A BIG DEAL WHEN PLUTO SHIFTS SIGNS
It signifies that a new quadrant of the Zodiac,
and therefore of human experience, is about to get an overhaul.

THE IMAGE FOR AQUARIUS IS THAT OF THE WATER BEARER
An angel from the heavens pours forth the nourishment of spiritual inspiration for all to receive. This manna is bestowed on each individual and so, the answer to all of the world's questions are spread out across the sea of humanity. As we move forwards it will be of growing importance to take heed and genuinely recognise the diversity of voices that make up our communities. A revolution of fairness and equality, not same-same but a genuine exploration of what each member in our community needs, physically as well as emotionally and spiritually. It may sound like an idealist's dream, but this is Aquarius that we are speaking of... and we are moving into the Aquarian Age.

PLUTO IS REFERRED TO AS THE LORD OF THE SHADES
He plows through the hidden lands of our individual and cultural subconscious, churning up buried motivations and weakness. As we walk towards our ideals, he highlights dysfunction and what needs to be transformed. We have a choice to address what's been exposed or be complicit in the corruption. Once you've seen and acknowledged a situation, you can't un-know it.

PLUTO HAS BEEN IN CAPRICORN SINCE 2008. HIS HAND CAN BE SEEN IN THE REALMS OF INSTITUTIONS, RULERS AND WORLD POWER.

It began with the global financial crisis. Then the slow and steady mistrust and erosion of people in positions of power. It continued with the exposure of corruption and the repugnant hypocrisy and rumoured (and proven) habits of an elite that were formerly hidden. Institutions toppled along with old statues. As he left Capricorn in March of 2023, banks and the financial system teetered on the brink...

PLUTO IN AQUARIUS MARCH - JUNE 2023

Have you started noticing the signs? It began for me when there was a lot of talk about bots running social media accounts. Then came the ads for AI that can write, produce and post content for you. AI won a major arts award... and suddenly anyone with a few words and an inclination became an artist.

WE ARE ABOUT TO SEE TECHNOLOGY EXPLODE

An AI found a cure for a particular cancer in six weeks. Nobel Prize? It may happen. Every sector in our society is going to get a machine work over. It's coming for us as well. Are our phones, never far from hand, a step toward transhumanism? The advancing tech revolution is a type of evolution. At what point does it impact on us to the degree that we forget being a HUMAN is something special and inimitable.

CAN YOU RECOGNISE THE HUMAN VOICE?

How do you feel knowing it's an AI that's advising you on matters human? How do we trust our ears and eyes when deep fake videos can make anyone say anything? Can you recognise a human voice from the fakes?

WHAT IS A HUMAN BEING?

This is the true theme for Pluto's passage through Aquarius. I am more interested in your answers than mine... Perhaps we can have a conversation about this on one of those fancy tech platforms in the year ahead? I wonder how we will understand this question by the time Pluto leaves Aquarius in 2044?

ENACTING IDEALISM

- Listen for answers that emerge from deep within.
- Take note of solutions as they come to mind.
- Pay attention to where things are falling apart; check if it's necessary for your, and also our collective, renewal.
- Aid in the fall of failed systems by non participation.
- Imagine the shifts that will happen when we act in accordance with our deepest goals, and follow the genuine moral impulses that we feel?
- We may shudder at Pluto transits, but in reality he is a potent ally.

INSPIRATIONS & KNOWINGS ...

Transits

SUN CONJUNCT PLUTO

Hand in hand the Sun and Pluto take a breath. One step... and together they enter Aquarius. Here, Pluto's journey begins in earnest. Over the next month, Mercury, Venus and Mars will pass Pluto. Like a procession of guests at a christening, introducing themselves and marking the occasion with a gift.

Take a minute to see what the Sun illuminates as Pluto crosses. This is a potent moment. Don't burden your notes with excessive logic. What's the feeling - the theme that you are experiencing? Insights now may make sense in the future as you travel with Pluto through Aquarius.

The week ahead

M

T

W

T

F

S

S

The weekly transits

First Quarter Moon in Aries
Mercury leaves Shadow Zone
Sun conjunct Pluto
Pluto enters Aquarius
Sun enters Aquarius

MONDAY
15th JANUARY

morning

afternoon

MOON ENTERS ARIES
Toronto - 11.49pm

TUESDAY
16th JANUARY

morning

afternoon

MOON ENTERS ARIES
London - 4.49am, Sydney - 3.49pm

WEDNESDAY
17th JANUARY

morning

afternoon

1st QUARTER MOON
IN *Aries*
Toronto - 10.52pm

THURSDAY
18th JANUARY

morning

afternoon

1st QUARTER MOON
IN *Aries*
London - 3.52am, Sydney - 2.52pm

MOON ENTERS TAURUS
Toronto - 3.12pm, London - 8.12am, Sydney - 7.12pm

FRIDAY
19th JANUARY

morning

Caution - wolf moon

afternoon

SUN CONJUNCT PLUTO IN CAPRICORN, THEN IN AQUARIUS.
Heightened Influence today through to 22nd January

SATURDAY
20th JANUARY

morning

afternoon

MOON ENTERS GEMINI
Toronto - 8.58am, London - 1.58pm

MERCURY LEAVES SHADOW ZONE

PLUTO ENTERS AQUARIUS
Toronto - 7.57pm

SUN ENTERS AQUARIUS
Toronto - 9.08am, London - 2.08pm

SUNDAY
21st JANUARY

morning

afternoon

MOON ENTERS GEMINI
Sydney - 12.58am

PLUTO ENTERS AQUARIUS
London - 12.57pm, Sydney - 11.57am

SUN ENTERS AQUARIUS
Toronto - 9.08am, London - 2.08pm, Sydney - 1.08am

SUN IN AQUARIUS
In the Land of Big Ideas

THE ELEVENTH HOUSE - FIXED AIR
PLANETARY RULER - SATURN & URANUS

Toronto 20th January - 18th February
London 20th January - 19th February
Sydney 21st January - 19th February

The Sun shines its light through the cool shimmering of Aquarius and the big ideas come into play. Perhaps none bigger than the weighty question, Why can't we all just get along?

We are a family, all we Humans, and well, just about every family I know has complex, convoluted and epic stories, so amplify that by... everyone on the planet. We are all interconnected. Where one suffers, so do we all.

The loftiest of minds have tried to work out how we can have a brighter, fairer, and more just world. How do we take care of our own needs and also meet the needs of others? Aquarius places the emphasis on OTHERS. Beyond borders, beyond familial ties, beyond class, race or gender.

But here's the challenge - society is made up of individuals who conform to their own patterns and dictates. Genuine change is slow. Enforced change, where an elect elite think they know best, leads to tyranny. Political correctness pushed too far leads to a type of socially-enforced totalitarianism. Both allow no room for the genuinely-quirky Human Being that the Water Bearer inspires.

So how do we move forward? I would suggest with hope and excitement, but also, with patience. Keep your eyes on the prize; influence by actioning the change you want to see in the world. Be wary of those who want you to plug into their ideology. Listen, but think for yourself and double check for any dogmas that may have snuck unawares into your own thinking.

Beware of corporations that want to plug you into their crap-i-verse where you get buffered about by algorithms beyond your influence. Participate, if you're curious, but remember that all online adventures mimic a combination of the rich and vast planet we live on, and our boundless internal lives.

Aquarius speaks to us of a World that is created by Humans
working together in freedom towards a common goal for the good.
What is more exciting than that?

Aquarius season
CONSIDERATIONS

Am I comfortable being myself, or do I feel a pressure to conform?
Do I allow those around me to be themselves,
or do I need them to fit into my worldview?
What are my big dreams for Humanity?
Any other questions or thoughts?

....

....

....

....

VENUS

IN *Capricorn*

Toronto, London 23rd January - 16th February
Sydney 23rd January - 17th February

THE MUSE

Venus works in the sphere of love, desire, creativity and relationships.
She influences our personal magnetism, tastes and resources.

LOVE AND DESIRE

To earn her trust, be on time. Stay true to your word. No excuses.
Surprise her with an upgrade in any area. Understand, her need for security
is not a ploy to trap you. She just doesn't want to waste her time.
Respect is key – and if you aren't showing up in your own life,
don't expect her to show up in yours.

CREATIVITY AND INSPIRATION

Commemorative monoliths, rambling fortress castles on hill tops, the
penthouse of an art deco skyscraper... She is inspired by a lasting legacy –
the mysterious way that value passes through the ages; the way a gem is
formed in the earth over millennia, transformed, faceted and set in gold.
A lineage of activity reaches through time, coming to rest as a beautiful
necklace that now adorns her.

THE MANNER OF RELATING

Venus can be quite the Queen. You'll treat her like one on the weight of her
willforce alone. She knows her value. She knows yours as well, even when
you might not see it yourself. She's canny... and funny (in the wise way of
those who know the seriousness of life).

Committed – Obsessive
Goal Oriented – Blind Ambition
Emotionally Mature – Cold and Cranky

I'M SO INSPIRED BY... I LOVE...
IT DRIVES ME CRAZY WHEN...
EXPLORE WHEN THE MOOD STRIKES

FULL MOON

Leo

PEAK ENERGY,
BLESSINGS & BLOSSOMS

25th January - Toronto 12.54pm, London 5.54pm
26th January - Sydney 4.54am

The Sun lays claim to the light of the Full Moon; isn't it his radiance reflected back at him? In mirroring, magic has occurred and he can now feel himself in the dark sky, a place his light doesn't allow him to linger. We too can catch glimpses of ourselves mirrored back to us by those around us.

We may feel pleased when it's the good and noble reflected, but when it's something less attractive that's hidden in the shadows (even from ourselves), it can be confronting. There's an instinct to reject this reflection in an effort to shuck the shadow right off of us like a burdensome monster.

You may have picked up that Pluto is involved with this full moon. Watch the drama unfold: Is it yours? Are you the audience? What is being mirrored back to you? Our shadow self wants to be brought into consciousness. Behold it. To know oneself is empowering.

HOW HAVE INTENTIONS MADE ON THE NEW MOON MANIFESTED?

....

....

....

The week ahead

M

T

W

T

F

S

S

The weekly transits

Sun enters Aquarius
Venus enters Capricorn
Full Moon in Leo

morning

afternoon

**MOON ENTERS
CANCER**
Toronto - 4.51pm, London - 9.51pm

TUESDAY
23rd JANUARY

morning

afternoon

**MOON ENTERS
CANCER**
Sydney - 8.51am

**VENUS ENTERS
CAPRICORN**
Toronto - 3.51pm, London - 8.51pm,
Sydney - 7.51am

WEDNESDAY
24th JANUARY

morning

afternoon

NEW MOON IN *Aries*
Sydney 4.22 am

home, family, housing

THURSDAY
25th JANUARY

morning

Wolf moon
- Fullness
- Completion
- drama
- Manifestation
- fruition

afternoon

Pluto explosive
hide under a
rock 19 → rest
of month

FRIDAY
26th JANUARY

morning

afternoon

FULL MOON IN *Leo*
Toronto - 12.54pm, London - 5.54am

FULL MOON IN *Leo*
Sydney - 4.54am

SATURDAY
27th JANUARY

morning

Triad -
expansint
luck

afternoon

Other people's
money.

SUNDAY
28th JANUARY

morning

afternoon

MOON ENTERS VIRGO
Toronto - 2.12pm, London - 7.12pm

MOON ENTERS VIRGO
Sydney - 6.12am

3rd QUARTER MOON

Scorpio

REFLECT & RELEASE

2nd February - Toronto 6.19pm, London 11.19pm
3rd February - Sydney 10.19am

What needs to be released? Fatigue? Stress? Emotional or financial burdens? It's time to let go. Your waking mind can't always be the part that's in control – it doesn't always allow room for the gifts that the cosmos bestows. Can't even see them sometimes... tricks us into thinking we created it all ourselves. Venus in Capricorn is supporting us with her grounded wisdom. Neptune and Uranus, together in Taurus, have a gift for us. Rest and receive.

WHAT HAVE I ACHIEVED
AND WHAT DO I NEED TO RELEASE?

....

....

....

....

....

....

....

THOUGHTS & INSIGHTS

The week ahead

M ....

T ....

W ....

T ....

F ....

S ....

S ....

The weekly transits

Third Quarter Moon in Scorpio
The Procession – Mercury
conjunct Pluto in Aquarius

MONDAY
29th JANUARY

morning

....
....
....
....
....

afternoon

....
....
....
....
....
....
....
....
....
....

TUESDAY
30th JANUARY

morning

afternoon

WEDNESDAY
31st JANUARY

morning

afternoon

MOON ENTERS LIBRA
Toronto - 3.04am,
London - 8.04am, Sydney - 7.04pm

THURSDAY
1st FEBRUARY

morning

Discipline
Focus
Action

afternoon

FRIDAY
2nd FEBRUARY

morning

afternoon

3rd QUARTER MOON

IN *Scorpio*

Toronto - 6.19pm, London - 11.19pm

Talking → visibility, mental energy

SATURDAY
3rd FEBRUARY

take action

SUNDAY
4th FEBRUARY

morning

morning

afternoon

afternoon

Networking, money.

3rd QUARTER MOON

IN *Scorpio*

Sydney - 10.19am

finance, education

MOON ENTERS
SAGITTARIUS

Toronto - 1.28am, London - 6.28am,
Sydney - 5.28pm

MERCURY

IN *Aquarius*

Toronto, London, Sydney 5th February - 23rd February

THE MESSENGER

Mercury influences how we transmit and receive information, our ideas and conversations as well as influencing movement, trade and travel.

The big ideas (the ones that change us and thereby the World) don't need to be complex – they need to be true. They can be as modest as a small seed in the palm of your hand. From that seed grows the tree – and likewise the simple truth will expand in us, as we meet it... This truth will take on new, individualised meanings in the soul of everyone it interacts with – just like how a tree grows according to its environment.

So what truth are you hearing at the moment? Are others hearing it? Can you recognise 'their truth' even though it differs from yours? While Mercury is in Aquarius we are encouraged to follow ideas back to their seed essence – perhaps we agree more than we differ?

Truth Seeking – Fixed Obstinance
Inclusivity – Exclusion
Holistic Perspective – Antisocial Behaviour

Obsession, excitement
transformation birth &
re-birth. 2008 - Now
pluto not in good angle
for Libra. Pluto good
sign. Re-ignite passion.
Bucket list.

Transits

The Procession Past Pluto Continues
MERCURY CONJUNCT PLUTO IN AQUARIUS

2nd - 9th February
Heightened Influence 5th through 7th February

There have alway been charlatans, charismatic tricksters and scammers. When we said yes to the World Wide Web and decided to cast a net around the globe a slew of portals opened, and through they came whistling.

Mercury is amped up when he partners with Pluto. He doesn't attack like Mars, but one still feels defeated by the onslaught of information... and disinformation. How to hear the tone of the trickster and decipher the ringing bell of a genuine opportunity? Fortunately this combination is perfect for in-depth research into the shadow zones. If you start to feel a bit manic or overwhelmed, retreat to the silence... seek it out if it's not immediately available.

NEW MOON

Aquarius

PLANTING SEEDS

9th February - Toronto 5.57pm, London 10.57pm
10th February - Sydney 9.57am

Just because something has always been done a certain way, doesn't make it the best way to do it. When custom and routine become dogma, it's time for a shake up, or at the very least, to question why we all agreed to go along this way in the first place.

At times, change takes courage – in this instance it involves listening to the most rational voice (internal or otherwise) and agreeing to move forwards with the best idea, the one that serves the good of the group. Most of us are willing to sacrifice an inch for the betterment of all – just be sure it's an idea in line with your deepest ideals.

New Moon in Aquarius themes: Community consciousness, idealism, activism for the common good, innovation and technology.

NEW MOON INTENTIONS

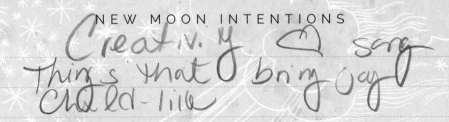

Creativity ♡ song
Things that bring joy
Child-like

The week ahead

M ....

T ....

W ....

T ....

F ....

S ....

S ....

MONDAY
5th FEBRUARY

morning
....
....
....
....

afternoon
....
....
....
....

MERCURY ENTERS AQUARIUS
Toronto - 12.10am,
London - 5.10am, Sydney - 4.10pm

MERCURY CONJUNCT PLUTO IN AQUARIUS
Heightened Influence today
though to 7th February

The weekly transits

Mercury conjunct Pluto
Mercury enters Aquarius
New Moon in Aquarius

TUESDAY
6th FEBRUARY

morning

afternoon

WEDNESDAY
7th FEBRUARY

morning

happy

afternoon

MOON ENTERS
CAPRICORN
Toronto - 7.09am,
London - 12.09pm, Sydney - 11.09pm

Power behind a group, friendship

THURSDAY
8th FEBRUARY

morning

✳ *Jdt*

afternoon

FRIDAY
9th FEBRUARY

morning

✳ *Manifestation*

Jan 27 → May 2
planets direct
Jan 21 - March 20
Unique & Uncommon

afternoon

MOON ENTERS
AQUARIUS
Sydney - 1.00am

NEW MOON IN
Aquarius
Toronto - 5.57pm, London - 10.57pm

MOON ENTERS
AQUARIUS
Toronto - 9.00am, London - 2.00pm

Social connection, technology.

SATURDAY
10th FEBRUARY

morning

afternoon

NEW MOON IN

Aquarius

Sydney - 9.57am

MOON ENTERS
PISCES
Toronto - 8.43am, London - 1.43pm

SUNDAY
11th FEBRUARY

morning

afternoon

MOON ENTERS
PISCES
Sydney - 12.43am

1st QUARTER MOON

Taurus

MOMENTUM & GROWTH

16th February - Toronto 10.15am, London 3.15pm
17th February - Sydney 2.01am

No doubt, the party is on over in Aquarius, Venus is set to join any minute. Thank the Gods for this Moon in Taurus – reminding us that we aren't just zapping synapses and brains walking about.

The Taurean Moon brings us back into our bodies, reminding us they have their own set of needs: nourishment, care, love and respect. Ideas may whizz about, but it takes someone to build, finance and manifest them. That person is priceless.

WHAT ACTIONS AM I TAKING TO FULFIL INTENTIONS SET ON THE NEW MOON?

Un common stars

MARS

IN *Aquarius*

Toronto 14th February - 22nd March
London 14th February - 23rd March
Sydney 15th February - 23rd March

THE WARRIOR

Mars works through our drives and desires; our ambitions
and how we achieve them. He sets and secures our personal boundaries
and defends us against those who transgress them.

DRIVES AND DESIRES

Mars in Aquarius is driven by an altruistic need to help better the planet for all.
His social instinct is refined and high minded. He builds social connections and
enters into conversations with ease and a touch of quirky humour.

AMBITION AND WORK

He works well in humanitarian, progressive and community-based projects.
You will also find his influence in the technology area – researching and
developing products that can be of assistance (be it renewable energy, medical
devices or solutions to pollution). He needs to believe in what he's doing.

BOUNDARIES AND PROTECTION

Mars in Aquarius is a giver not a fighter. But if you breach his boundaries
you'll either get frozen out for a while or he'll just disappear altogether.
Absence is the teacher here – he'll feel no need to justify his reasons to you.

*When Mars is in Aquarius you may experience: Physical endurance,
a strong will, an altruistic attitude, a heightened capacity
for self-motivation and self-reliance.*

*Difficulties you may encounter: Self-doubt, workaholism, isolationism,
blind ambition and a need to control the world around you.*

VENUS

IN *Aquarius*

Toronto, London 16th February - 11th March
Sydney 17th February - 12th March

THE MUSE
Venus works in the sphere of love, desire, creativity and relationships.
She influences our personal magnetism, tastes and resources.

LOVE AND DESIRE
Venus in Aquarius values longevity in relationships. She is wise in her
knowing that love's bloom can fade but a deeply-committed friendship
can last a lifetime. Nurturing the roots, enables spring blossoms to flourish.

CREATIVITY AND INSPIRATION
Think vistas of clouds, simulacrums of the heavens and science fiction
as a muse. Sustainable living meets high tech with a yen of low-brow
inventions that value-add and dissuade from boredom.

THE MANNER OF RELATING
Can you come to depend on unpredictability? She lives in an ever-changing
and flexible universe – but you may find that HER views can be quite fixed
(although she'll love you for holding onto yours). Her friendship circle is vast
and diverse; at times she may be the only common denominator.

Electrifying – Fixed
Friendly and Companionable – Isolated and Cold
Broadminded – Fixed

I'M SO INSPIRED BY... I LOVE...
IT DRIVES ME CRAZY WHEN...
EXPLORE WHEN THE MOOD STRIKES

Transits

The Procession Past Pluto Continues

MARS CONJUNCT PLUTO IN AQUARIUS

9th through 21st February
Heightened Influence 13th through 17th February

The ambition and drive of Mars meet Pluto and his indomitable will for power, leading to a burning need for action. Be aware that we are all going through these intense transits, some with no awareness of the cosmic pressure being applied. You may feel a deep anger emerging or encounter eruptions in your environment. If you are experiencing too much pressure, step back, process and wait for decompression.

If you need to make big changes this energy will back you, but remember, whatever Pluto touches can leave a radioactive trace; it would be wise to act with awareness and tact.

VENUS CONJUNCT PLUTO IN AQUARIUS

13th through 22nd February
Heightened Influence 15th through 18th February

As Pluto shifted into Aquarius during March of 2023 a new type of filter was released. The dodgy 'green screen' moments were gone and in came machine learning. An AI scans the 'most desirable' elements of thousands of women's faces and then superimposes bits of them over yours in real time. You look a little like yourself, but fashioned into the consensus of the 'beauty type' of the day.

It's like there's a female demon that crushes a woman into a thousand pieces when they can't achieve her proportions – that demoness has been haunting these halls a long time. She's a shapeshifter. You'll never have her face no matter how much you cut up or cover up yours. And that woman – no matter how perfect she seems to be, lives in fear the mask will slip. Because it will. That's called time.

Can you be radically, uniquely, spectacularly you? Can you fight the programming? Can you stand up for the quirks in others and let them know they are loved? If this doesn't affect you, check in with your daughter, your sister, friends and loved ones. Men also. Male immunity isn't guaranteed.

The week ahead

M

....

T

....

W

....

T

....

F

....

S

....

S

....

The weekly transits

Mars enters Aquarius
Venus enters Aquarius
The procession - Mars conjunct
Pluto in Aquarius
Venus conjunct Pluto in Aquarius

morning

....

....

....

....

afternoon

....

....

....

....

....

....

....

....

....

MOON ENTERS ARIES

Toronto - 8.26, London - 1.26pm

TUESDAY
13th FEBRUARY

morning

Dreamy/
romantic
Big purchase

afternoon

WEDNESDAY
14th FEBRUARY

morning

afternoon

MOON ENTERS ARIES
Sydney - 12.26am

MARS ENTERS AQUARIUS
Toronto - 10.03am, London - 3.03pm

morning

morning

Jd

afternoon

afternoon

MARS ENTERS AQUARIUS
Sydney - 2.03am

VENUS CONJUNCT PLUTO IN AQUARIUS
Heightened Influence today
though to 18th February

MARS CONJUNCT PLUTO IN AQUARIUS
Heightened Influence today
though to 17th February

1st QUARTER MOON
IN *Taurus*
Toronto - 10.01am, London - 3.01pm

VENUS ENTERS AQUARIUS
Toronto - 11.05am, London - 4.05pm

MOON ENTERS GEMINI
Toronto - 2.40pm, London - 7.40pm

SATURDAY
17th FEBRUARY

morning

....

....

....

....

afternoon

....

....

....

1st QUARTER MOON
IN *Taurus*
Sydney - 2.01am

**VENUS ENTERS
AQUARIUS**
Sydney - 3.05am

**MOON ENTERS
GEMINI**
Sydney - 6.40am

SUNDAY
18th FEBRUARY

morning

....

....

....

....

afternoon

....

....

....

....

SUN IN PISCES

The Land of Dreams & Grace

THE TWELFTH HOUSE - MUTABLE WATER
PLANETARY RULER - JUPITER & NEPTUNE

Toronto 18th February - 20th March
London, Sydney 19th February - 20th March

The Sun shines through the mists of Pisces. So curious that the holidays are behind us. It's time to let go of all control freakery, self-imposed or otherwise. We're in the New Year, almost used to saying 2024, back in the hurry of life. Astrologically and energetically speaking, however, we are in the wrap-up season.

Enough with the hustle! What's needed is time to digest, rest and metabolise. When we push and push through fatigue and exhaustion we are asking our bodies for an advance. We'll be paying for it sometime in the future.

This Pisces season, go with whatever opportunities present themselves around rest and recuperation. Gently put off the hurriers and pushers. If possible, say yes to bodywork and healing sessions...

Sift through any ancient stories that emerge from the depths of your emotional world. Perhaps start that lucid dreaming practice you have been thinking of, or sing more, dance more. Walk in the wilderness and find refuge in the unpolluted spaces – places where it's safe for the mind to expand and dream.

Talk with your soul family, those who speak in your particular type of code. Spend time with your tribe – in the forest, by the ocean or atop the highest building with the best view of the twinkling lights... Be open to spontaneity.

It's hard to control the Pisces season. The more you try, the slipperier things get. Like trying to catch fish barehanded. Trust in the cycle. Aries season is just around the corner and fresh energy will come flooding in as the new Astrological year begins.

Pisces season
CONSIDERATIONS

How do I calm my nervous system?
Where is my tribe? Who are my tribe?
Am I getting enough sleep?
Review the last 12 Months – just as you would around New Year's Eve.
How's the journey been?

MERCURY

IN *Pisces*

Toronto 23 February - 9th March
London, Sydney 23 February - 10th March

THE MESSENGER

Mercury influences how we transmit and receive information, our ideas and conversations as well as influencing movement, trade and travel.

Remember that dreams are also conversations – in reality isn't everything a type of communication? Scents drifting on the air tell us of flowers in bloom, a song opens up a world of mood and non-verbal cues awaken memories from slumbering depths. Glimpses of dreams snap into focus. Patterns appear and synchronicities open our hearts and set us pondering. It can be difficult to find words for the magical interface between our inner universe and the outer world, the way they meld and switch places...

Not everyone has the language to understand you. Some conversations are best saved for soul family. How do you know who your soul family are? They're the ones who listen, absorb and share ineffable, ethereal encounters of their own.

Realisations and Insights - Delusions
Intuition - Emotional Confusion
Empathy - Lack of Discernment

I'VE BEEN THINKING ABOUT...
I JUST WANT TO SAY...

FULL MOON

Virgo

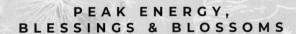

PEAK ENERGY,
BLESSINGS & BLOSSOMS

24th February - Toronto 7.32am,
London 12.32am, Sydney 11.32pm

She shines so sweetly, amidst her field of stars. All the other planets are clustered in the four constellations stretching from Aquarius through to Taurus. She's on the opposite end of the Heavens, holding her own. In much the same way, we may find ourselves holding a view, or shining a light that places us on the opposing side of the masses. They seem quite certain they are right – but just because everyone says it is so, is no guarantee it is for you.

There may be a lot of pressure to conform. Take the time you need to analyse the data and assess the situation for yourself. You may not be an expert, but we all have an inner moral compass. It's a sacred part of us, one that connects us to the Great All That Is. Listen. You'll know the answer and find the right action to take.

HOW HAVE INTENTIONS MADE ON THE NEW MOON MANIFESTED?

March 25 - eclipse cycle
hot seat 4-6 wks before &
after
Life changing things
2013-2015
    1995-1997 - birth
    Big beginnings / endings in
relationships

Intense

The week ahead

M

T

W

T

F

S

S

The weekly transits

Sun enters Pisces
Mercury enters Pisces
Full Moon in Virgo

morning

afternoon

MOON ENTERS CANCER
London - 3.25am, Sydney - 2.25pm

SUN ENTERS PISCES
London - 4.13am, Sydney - 3.13pm

Take advantage of this time

TUESDAY
20th FEBRUARY

morning

afternoon

WEDNESDAY
21st FEBRUARY

morning

afternoon

Lock in good long term gains,

MOON ENTERS LEO
Toronto - 8.41am, London - 1.41pm

THURSDAY
22nd FEBRUARY

morning

afternoon

MOON ENTERS LEO
Sydney - 12.41am

FRIDAY
23rd FEBRUARY

morning

afternoon

MERCURY ENTERS PISCES
Toronto - 3.29am,
London - 8.29am, Sydney - 7.39pm

SATURDAY
24th FEBRUARY

morning

afternoon

SUNDAY
25th FEBRUARY

morning

afternoon

FULL MOON IN *Virgo*
Toronto - 7.32am,
London - 12.32pm, Sydney - 11.32pm

3rd QUARTER MOON

Sagittarius

REFLECT & RELEASE

3rd March - Toronto 10.24am, London 3.24pm
4th March - Sydney 2.24am

Life can be exhausting. Do our bodies even know it's time to shut down and rest when our minds keep spinning on in an endless cycle of noise and activity? As the Moon's light ebbs and drains away, our drive and vitality can diminish with her. Take time to rest.

Even though the year is still just getting going, astrologically speaking, we are coming to the end of the yearly cycle, so don't go thinking you need to push through any fatigue that you may be experiencing. Exhaustion can be a profound teacher, is it quietly whispering to you:

WHAT HAVE I ACHIEVED
AND WHAT DO I NEED TO RELEASE?

Transits

THE NORTH NODE CONJUNCT CHIRON

17th January through 19th April
Heightened Influence 26th February through 15th March

This transit has a broad impact. It ripples through smaller groups and society at large. Chiron works painful pressure points with persistence, exposing suffering and encouraging healing. The North Node points to the future, that place that we never quite seem to get to. Combined they pose the questions: What does the future hold? How do we move forward in a healthy way? Crisis can shift to quest. If you are beset with anxiety, remember, one breath at a time, one day at a time...

SUN CONJUNCT SATURN IN PISCES

22nd February through 5th March
Heightened Influence 28th February through 2nd March

What was bestowed on you by the grandparents or elders in your life? What have you learnt from the way they lived their lives? How do you wish to age? One day, time will have snuck up and you'll pluck your first white hair. What wisdom will you impart? Are you proud of how you've sung your song and of the legacy you'll leave, one meeting at a time, imprinted on the soul of others?

The week ahead

M
....

T
....

W
....

T
....

F
....

S
....

S
....

morning

afternoon

The weekly transits

North Node conjunct Chiron
Sun conjunct Saturn in Pisces
Third Quarter Moon in Sagittarius

MOON ENTERS LIBRA
Toronto - 9.30pm, London - 2.30pm

THE NORTH NODE CONJUNCT CHIRON
Heightened Influence today
through to 15th March

TUESDAY
27th FEBRUARY

morning

afternoon

MOON ENTERS LIBRA
Sydney - 1.30am

WEDNESDAY
28th FEBRUARY

morning

afternoon

**MOON ENTERS
SCORPIO**
Toronto - 10.09pm

**SUN CONJUNCT
SATURN IN PISCES**
Heightened Influence today
through to 2nd March

THURSDAY
29th FEBRUARY

morning

afternoon

FRIDAY
1st MARCH

morning

afternoon

MOON ENTERS
SCORPIO
London - 3.09am, Sydney - 2.09pm

SATURDAY
2nd MARCH

morning

afternoon

SUNDAY
3rd MARCH

morning

afternoon

3rd QUARTER MOON
IN *Sagittarius*
Toronto - 10.24am, London - 3.24am

MERCURY

IN *Aries*

Toronto & London 23rd February - 15th March
Sydney 23rd February - 16th March

THE MESSENGER

Mercury influences how we transmit and receive information, our ideas and conversations as well as influencing movement, trade and travel.

The Sun, still in Pisces and with Venus just about to join, has us deep in the dreamtime. But here's Mercury, barrelling past the Aries point (the marker that signifies the beginning of the Astrological cycle) and our basking in a lingering dream is interrupted by excited conversation... the odd shout and hysterical, raucous laughter from the next room.

If I stick my head under the pillow will you all just go away? It may feel a little jarring, like: Why did I get a roommate? Mercury keeps blazing and Aries energy can't be blocked.

So, speak from the heart, say what you mean, trust that if words come out thick, fast and a touch blunt, it's the intention and the meaning they carry that matter. Spontaneous words convey what cautious hypervigilant words conceal. Listen for the magic of the new AND keep frolicking in the eternal Piscean ocean.

Honest - Insensitive
Quick Wits - Rudely Blunt
Clear and to the Point - Obnoxious

I'VE BEEN THINKING ABOUT...
I JUST WANT TO SAY...

NEW MOON

Pisces

PLANTING SEEDS

10th March - Toronto 3.59am,
London 8.59am, Sydney 7.59pm

Sun and Moon meet in the indigo sky.
Picture this: mountain streams, suburban gutters and small tributaries flow to the river, each carrying droplets of water imprinted with a diverse range of experiences. The river grows mighty, gathering the trillions of stories held within each droplet, on her way to meet the sea. The ocean roars, spits spray to the wind, pushes discarded plastic and driftwood alike onto the shore, rearranging the landscape with a dreamlike abandon.

This is where we are. Memories held in the waters of our bodies. The flotsam and jetsam of a cycle's worth of goings-on to sort through, to forgive and to forget. The year is ticking on and the calendar is telling us 2024, but the fire of Aries season (and the beginning of the astrological year) is just around the corner, so let's dwell a while in this Pisces wonderland as long as the Sun, Moon and Stars bid us.

New Moon in Pisces themes: Timelessness, compassion, being in the moment, spirituality, love without judgment, boundary issues.

NEW MOON INTENTIONS

....

....

....

Transits

MERCURY CONJUNCT NEPTUNE IN PISCES

6th March through 12th March
Heightened Influence 8th March through 10th March

Mercury gracefully approaches Neptune and if there was ever a moment to start speaking in tongues, this is it!
What would you say if you were possessed by the divine spirit?
What dreamscape might come rambling out?
Let it flow. There's extra magic in words these days.

The week ahead

M

T

W

T

F

S

S

MONDAY
4th MARCH

morning

afternoon

The weekly transits

Mercury enters Aries
Mercury conjunct Neptune in Pisces
New Moon in Pisces

3rd QUARTER MOON
in *Sagittarius*
Sydney - 2.24am

MOON ENTERS CAPRICORN
Toronto - 4.15pm, London - 9.15pm

TUESDAY
5th MARCH

morning

afternoon

**MOON ENTERS
CAPRICORN**

Sydney - 8.15 am

WEDNESDAY
6th MARCH

morning

afternoon

**MOON ENTERS
AQUARIUS**

Toronto - 12.03am

THURSDAY
7th MARCH

morning

afternoon

**MOON ENTERS
AQUARIUS**
London - 7.39pm, Sydney - 11.39am

FRIDAY
8th MARCH

morning

afternoon

MOON ENTERS PISCES
Toronto - 8.04pm

**MERCURY CONJUNCT
NEPTUNE IN PISCES**
Heightened Influence today
through to 18th March

SATURDAY
9th MARCH

morning

afternoon

MOON ENTERS PISCES
London - 1.04am, Sydney - 12.04pm

MERCURY ENTERS ARIES
Toronto - 11.03pm

SUNDAY
10th MARCH

morning

afternoon

NEW MOON IN *Pisces*
Toronto - 3.59am, London - 8.59am,
Sydney - 7.59pm

MERCURY ENTERS ARIES
London - 4.03am, Sydney - 3.03pm

MOON ENTERS ARIES
Toronto - 8.20pm

VENUS

IN *Pisces*

Toronto 11th March - 4th April
London 11th March - 5th April
Sydney 12th March - 5th April

THE MUSE

Venus works in the sphere of love, desire, creativity and relationships. She influences our personal magnetism, tastes and resources.

LOVE AND DESIRE

True love – the legend of twin souls travelling from spirit to earth and back in an endless cycle of loss and reunification; dissolving boundaries between ourselves and the other is the song sung by the twin fishes, who swim between the worlds.

CREATIVITY AND INSPIRATION

Atlantis beneath the waves, Neptune riding a White Sea foam horse and mermaids singing siren songs to lonely sailers at sea... Go with the flow – there is no realm of the imagination that doesn't already live inside you.

THE MANNER OF RELATING

Deeply empathic and compassionate – but like the slip silver of the moon reflected on the ocean, her pull is magnetic and as with a rip, you might get stuck out at sea. Flow with her, but don't get frustrated when she grows a tail and swims back out to sea. She needs room to follow her own muse.

Humorous and Playful – Scattered and Melodramatic
Sensual – Hypersensitive and Overly Dependent
Selfless and Generous – Lack of Discernment

I'M SO INSPIRED BY... I LOVE...
IT DRIVES ME CRAZY WHEN...
EXPLORE WHEN THE MOOD STRIKES

1st QUARTER MOON
Gemini

MOMENTUM & GROWTH

16th March - Toronto 12.10am
17th March - London 4.10am, Sydney 3.10pm

The Pisces dreamland continues to enthrall and possibly confuse;
the Sun is holding court with Neptune. Some of us are receiving
supreme visions and realisations direct from Spirit, whilst others
may have had their fill of 'reality' and turned to copious amounts of sugar,
the bottle or... name your addiction.

This Gemini Moon has suggestions on how to pull oneself out of a funk and
on how to ground your spiritual insights so they don't dissolve into pixie dust
once the 'real world' comes calling. Take notes.

WHAT ACTIONS AM I TAKING TO FULFIL INTENTIONS SET ON THE NEW MOON?

....

....

....

....

....

Transits

SUN CONJUNCT NEPTUNE IN PISCES

12th through 22nd March
Heightened Influence 15th through 19th March

Ah! Radiance of the Sun, warming us through as we flow with the currents and are swept on the waves. There is nothing to do but surrender to the journey. Release and dissolve all lingering cares and concerns. The astrological year begins in a few days, but for now, relax, sleep, rest and see what wants to be dreamt.

The week ahead

M

T

W

T

F

S

S

morning

afternoon

The weekly transits

Venus in Pisces
First Quarter Moon in Gemini
Sun conjunct Neptune in Pisces

MOON ENTERS ARIES
London - 12.20am, Sydney - 11.20am

VENUS ENTERS PISCES
Toronto - 5.51pm, London - 9.51pm

TUESDAY
12th MARCH

morning

afternoon

**VENUS ENTERS
PISCES**
Sydney - 8.51am

**MOON ENTERS
TAURUS**
Toronto - 8.29pm

WEDNESDAY
13th MARCH

morning

afternoon

**MOON ENTERS
TAURUS**
London - 12.29am, Sydney - 11.29pm

THURSDAY
14th MARCH

morning

afternoon

**MOON ENTERS
GEMINI**
Toronto - 11.16pm

FRIDAY
15th MARCH

morning

afternoon

**MOON ENTERS
GEMINI**
London - 3.16am, Sydney - 2.16pm

**SUN CONJUNCT
NEPTUNE IN PISCES**
Heightened Influence today
through to 19th March

SATURDAY
16th MARCH

morning

afternoon

SUNDAY
17th MARCH

morning

afternoon

1st QUARTER MOON
IN *Gemini*

Toronto - 12.10am, London - 4.10am,
Sydney - 3.10pm

MOON ENTERS CANCER

Toronto - 5.41am, London - 9.41am,
Sydney - 8.41pm

A New Beginning

THE FIRST HOUSE - CARDINAL FIRE
PLANETARY RULER - MARS

Toronto, London 19th March - 19th April
Sydney 20th March - 20th April

Aries season is here and with it the beginning of a new Astrological cycle. New energy incoming - and if you are not feeling it yet, well, it waits for no one.

You may find your calendar filling up with appointments and engagements pulling you out of the quiet nook you've been lodged in. Give it a week or so and watch as your life gains a new momentum. Say YES! Did ever a new adventure begin with 'no, not ready yet'?

Aries energy is potent. It is the rising Sun that chases the night things from the garden, driving away heaviness and damp. It fills our bodies with the energy to burst from the bed each morning with enthusiasm enough for a world of tasks - it pushes the plant from the safety of the seeds kernel.

They say destiny favours the bold and Aries nods in full agreement. Aries energy encourages us to step up and show up in our lives. To take charge and follow through on our plans with drive, discipline, willpower and stamina. Does this sound intimidating or exhausting? That's the push of Mars that you're feeling. He's always seeking to breakthrough and this is his time.

If you are having difficulty connecting with the vital Aries energy I suggest meditating on the seed pushing through the husk - focus on the force behind the image and then see if you can feel where this energy lives in you. What drives and inspires new growth in your being?

Aries season

CONSIDERATIONS

Are the goals I set at New Years on track?
Are they relevant? Any revisions?
How is my physical stamina?
What type of exercise suits me and do I do enough?

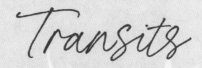

Transits

VENUS CONJUNCT SATURN IN PISCES

18th through 27th March
Heightened Influence 20th through 25th March

Wizened age and experience has a lot to teach youthful beauty. There are dangers along the path of life. How often did we actually listen to the advice and heed the warnings of our elders? Did we just brush them of with a secret inner assurance that they just never really knew what it was like to fall in love and feel the sensuous delights of this world? Saturn's over cautiousness and Venus's lack of any make for an interesting outcome...

MERCURY CONJUNCT CHIRON IN ARIES

18th through 26th March
Heightened Influence 20th through 23rd March

The kids are not ok. Schools are losing teachers to overwhelm and exhaustion in droves. The numbers of male teachers have been whittled down yet half the students are boys. Who do they have to look up to - if they look up from their device at all. Our children are the expression of humanity as a whole, they don't have the facility to disguise and repress their sadness, confusion and rage. Embrace the conversations, show up, be there for them. How might you engage them to seek solutions together?

MARS

IN *Pisces*

Toronto 22nd March – 30th April
London 23rd March – 30th April
Sydney 23rd March – 1st May

THE WARRIOR

Mars works through our drives and desires; our ambitions
and how we achieve them. He sets and secures our personal boundaries
and defends us against those who transgress them.

DRIVES AND DESIRES

Mars in Pisces is driven to experiences that lift him out of a mundane reality.
This is Mars coloured by Jupiter and Neptune - He seeks spiritual experience,
depending on your own nature you'll feel this as a pull towards philosophy and
a disciplined practise or you'll seek out substances to escape the doldrums.

AMBITION AND WORK

Thoughtful and dreamy, Mars isn't in a hurry to get the task done.
He is highly imaginative and considerate and works well with colleagues.

BOUNDARIES AND PROTECTION

In Pisces we experience the disintegration of the egoist aspect of our nature
- it's the place where hard edges get smoothed and where we feel every sigh
and heave of the collective. Mars wants those boundaries tight, but he is
fighting the mists. He can't quite make out what is you and what is me - what
is his and what is hers. Once he learns however, his fine senses are keenly
attuned to cues that would be missed by straighter shooters.

*When Mars is in Pisces you may experience: Intuition and inspiration in
activity, a yen for novel encounters and heightened sensitivity.*

*Difficulties you may encounter: Fatigue, self-doubt, loss of ambition and will
power and a feeling it's all out of our hands.*

The week ahead

M

T

W

T

F

S

S

The weekly transits

Sun enters Aries
Venus conjunct Saturn in Pisces
Mercury conjunct Chiron in Aries
Mars enters Pisces

morning

afternoon

TUESDAY
19th MARCH

morning

afternoon

SUN ENTERS ARIES
Toronto - 11.06pm

WEDNESDAY
20th MARCH

morning

afternoon

SUN ENTERS ARIES
London - 3.06am, Sydney - 2.06pm

**VENUS CONJUNCT
SATURN IN PISCES**
Heightened Influence today
through 25th March

**MERCURY CONJUNCT
CHIRON IN ARIES**
Heightened Influence today
through 23rd March

THURSDAY
21st MARCH

morning

afternoon

**MOON ENTERS
VIRGO**
Toronto - 3.42am

FRIDAY
22nd MARCH

morning

afternoon

**MOON ENTERS
VIRGO**
London - 7.42pm, Sydney - 6.42pm

**MARS ENTERS
PISCES**
Toronto - 7.47pm

afternoon

afternoon

MARS ENTERS
PISCES
London - 11.47am, Sydney - 10.47am

FULL MOON
Libra

PENUMBRAL LUNAR ECLIPSE
THE DOOR IS AJAR

25th March - Toronto 3am, London 7am,
Sydney 6pm

This isn't a full eclipse, but the door is ajar and a little chaos is freed to run amok. The Aries Sun is holding fort for individual rights and the Libran Moon whispers, 'but what about us?'

There's a quiet urgency to this question as Mars and Pluto are both activated. How do we walk the path we've forged alone and the road our relationships want us to travel down? Between my rights to do as I please, to say what I want and the cultural atmosphere of the times that cautions when it sees a peek of genuine self expression. Just like an old fashioned see-saw it's all in the balance, there's a rhythm to the up and down. Sometimes we find ourselves totally met and suspended in a moment of equilibrium, we catch the lesson and lean into the process all over again.

For the next two weeks we are in eclipse season - watch for unexpected occurrences and visits. What or whom will come through the eclipse portal?

HOW HAVE INTENTIONS MADE
ON THE NEW MOON MANIFESTED?

_____

_____

_____

Transits

VENUS CONJUNCT NEPTUNE IN PISCES

30th March through 8th April
Heightened Influence 2nd through 6th April

If you feel the sensitive tendrils of your heart's yearning begin to awaken, allow yourself to follow the tune. Inspiration doesn't flow through closed channels and unless we become aware of what is that we truly seek, will we recognise it when it appears?

JUPITER CONJUNCT URANUS IN TAURUS

24th March through 22nd May
Heightened Influence 27th March through 1st May
Exact conjunction 18th through 25th April

This transit spans a period of two months - it's slow moving and is powerfully reshaping the world around us. A Human lifespan is a single breath when compared to the great swathes of time that the mineral kingdom breathes through. The intricacies of our ancestors' lives fade to a few remembered passages, passed down in a sequence of whispers that blur, just a little with each telling. But the Earth, she has her own way of storing the memories of those who walked her gardens. Jupiter and Uranus coming together in the most fixed of earth signs seek to wrangle loose wisdom forgotten by us, but held tightly by the King of the Mountains and the Lady of the Vale.
Be open to revelation at this time. Deep truths and memories are emerging from the bog, the meadow, the crystals and the hills. The great earth Mother is stirring and stretching - did we forget that she is a living being as well?

The week ahead

M

T

W

T

F

S

S

The weekly transits

Penumbral Luna Eclipse -
Full Moon in Libra
Venus conjunct Neptune in Pisces
Jupiter conjunct Uranus in Taurus -
A slow building two month transit

morning

afternoon

**PENUMBRAL
LUNA ECLIPSE -
FULL MOON IN**
Libra
Toronto - 3am, London - 7am,
Sydney - 6pm

TUESDAY
26th MARCH

morning

afternoon

WEDNESDAY
27th MARCH

morning

afternoon

MOON ENTERS
SCORPIO
Toronto - 5.03am, London - 9.03am,
Sydney - 8.03 pm

THURSDAY
28th MARCH

morning

afternoon

FRIDAY
29th MARCH

morning

afternoon

MOON ENTERS SAGITTARIUS
Toronto - 3.52pm, London - 7.52pm

SATURDAY
30th MARCH

morning

afternoon

**MOON ENTERS
SAGITTARIUS**
Sydney - 6.52 am

**VENUS CONJUNCT
NEPTUNE IN PISCES**
Heightened Influence today
though 6th April

SUNDAY
31st MARCH

morning

afternoon

**3rd QUARTER MOON
IN *Capricorn***
Toronto - 11.24am, London - 3.24pm

3rd QUARTER MOON

Capricorn

FINDING STEADY FOOTING -
THE SPACE BETWEEN ECLIPSES

31st March Toronto 11.24am, London 4.24pm
1st April Sydney 2.24am

Whatever lunacy might be whirling about, somehow, under the tutelage
of the Capricorn Moon we can find an anchor. Saturn is also offering a
steadying hand. But still, it may feel as if the boat of life is listing.
What would happen if you stayed still and simply observed the storms
around you? The Moon is slowly walking her way towards next week's total
Solar Eclipse and as she does we may find our energies starting to flag.
Rest and recuperate and choose wisely if you start getting the urge
to chase any storms.

WHAT HAVE I ACHIEVED
AND WHAT DO I NEED TO RELEASE?

MERCURY RETROGRADE

in *Aries*

1st April through until the 13th May
Toronto - Retrograde 1st April, Direct 25th April, Leaves Shadow Zone 13th May
London - Retrograde 1st April, Direct 25th April, Leaves Shadow Zone 14th May
Sydney - Retrograde 2nd April, Direct 25th April, Leaves Shadow Zone 14th May

Mercury retro! It's become a popular catch-line.
Why? Perhaps because wires really do get crossed, electronics can suddenly short and communications can go awry and sometimes, bite. A lot gets blamed on Mercury retro - but it certainly isn't a curse.
General rule of thumb is to avoid signing contracts, releasing projects and anything else where easy, clean momentum is desired.

The less acknowledged side to Mercury retro, is the pause in the breakneck pace of duties fulfilled and ambitions pursued. You may feel inclined to turn inwards and reflect - when you hit a roadblock you turn around and find another way - is there a better approach to how you conduct your affairs? Do you always know best? Is there someone you've brushed off with frustration or haste that requires a conversation? The Aries element can be a little stubborn, single focused and hard headed at times.

Just as Mercury pivots to backwards - Venus comes charging into Aries. Watch for the juxtaposition of 'what the heart wants it gets' - it's an unconscious entitled vibe versus the 'we need to talk about what just happened' reflective clean up type of conversation.

Look for interruptions to plans and projects, adventures and quite possibly your alone time, space and privacy.

VENUS

IN *Aries*

Toronto, London, Sydney 5th - 29th April

THE MUSE

Venus works in the sphere of love, desire, creativity and relationships.
She influences our personal magnetism, tastes and resources.

LOVE AND DESIRE

Venus in Aries comes in hot and focused, she knows what she likes
and can recognise it instantly. Equally, she knows what she hates
and can be quick to judge.

CREATIVITY AND INSPIRATION

To connect with Venus in Aries, get moving. Take a trip, a hike,
buy a bike - that feeling of wind on your face as you cut through space
is the air she breathes.

THE MANNER OF RELATING

There is something eternally youthful about her. She's playful and present,
her enthusiasm is catching and you can trust her words - as blunt as they
may be. It's charming, the way she knows herself and admits when she's
misjudged and been too hasty to condemn.
Mistakes aren't malevolence, there is something impetuous
and childlike about her.

Quick to love - Quick to hate
Focused - Hard headed
Takes things into her own hands - Indiscriminate

I'M SO INSPIRED BY... I LOVE...
IT DRIVES ME CRAZY WHEN...
EXPLORE WHEN THE MOOD STRIKES

The week ahead

M

T

W

T

F

S

S

The weekly transits

Third Quarter Moon in Capricorn
Mercury Retrograde in Aries
Venus enters Aries

morning

afternoon

**MERCURY
RETROGRADE IN
ARIES**
Toronto - 6.14pm, London - 11.14pm

TUESDAY
2nd APRIL

morning

afternoon

3rd QUARTER MOON
IN *Capricorn*
Sydney - 2.24am

MERCURY RETROGRADE IN ARIES
Sydney - 9.13am

WEDNESDAY
3rd APRIL

morning

afternoon

MOON ENTERS AQUARIUS
Toronto - 5.08am,
London - 10.08am, Sydney - 8.08pm

THURSDAY
4th APRIL

morning

afternoon

FRIDAY
5th APRIL

morning

afternoon

MOON ENTERS PISCES
Toronto - 7.13am, London - 12.13pm,
Sydney - 10.13pm

JUPITER CONJUNCT URANUS IN TAURUS
Heightened influence today
through 5th May

VENUS ENTERS ARIES
Toronto - 12am, London - 5am,
Sydney - 3pm

SATURDAY
6th APRIL

morning

afternoon

SUNDAY
7th APRIL

morning

afternoon

MOON ENTERS ARIES
Toronto - 7.25am, London - 11.25am,
Sydney - 9.25 pm

NEW MOON

Aries

TOTAL SOLAR ECLIPSE - CONJUNCT CHIRON

IN THE SHADOW OF THE MOON

8th April Toronto - 2.19am, London - 7.19am
9th April - Sydney - 4.19pm

In a Solar Eclipse the Moon blocks the light of the Sun and the dark side of the Moon is fully lit. It's like we are out of the conversation, thrown back on our own devices without the radiant guidance of the Sun.

As it occurs in Aries, themes around our individuality and vital forces come to the forefront and this is especially heightened as the Eclipse occurs on the same degree as Chiron. What lessons are you being shown? Chiron always offers a key, a way through suffering - a guiding thought, experience or encounter that shows you a previously obscured path forwards.
Do you feel safe being yourself? Are you able to speak your mind without fear of ostracisation and misunderstanding? How is your life force and vital energy - If you are challenged how might you support yourself?
This is the only Solar Eclipse visible in Mexico, America and Canada in the entire 21st Century.

THE ECLIPSE PORTAL WHICH HAS BEEN OPEN FOR THE LAST TWO WEEKS GRADUALLY CLOSES. WHAT HAS ENTERED YOUR LIFE? WHO OR WHAT HAS LEFT?

THOUGHTS & INSIGHTS

The week ahead

M

T

W

T

F

S

S

The weekly transits

Mars conjunct Saturn in Pisces
New Moon in Aries - Total Solar
Eclipse - conjunct Chiron

morning

afternoon

**MARS CONJUNCT
SATURN IN PISCES**
Heightened today
though 16th April

TUESDAY
9th APRIL

morning

afternoon

WEDNESDAY
10th APRIL

morning

afternoon

NEW MOON IN
Aries - TOTAL
SOLAR ECLIPSE -
CONJUNCT CHIRON
Toronto - 2.19am, London - 7.19am,
Sydney - 4.19 pm

MOON ENTERS
TAURUS
Toronto - 9am, London - 2pm,
Sydney - 11pm

THURSDAY
11th APRIL

morning

afternoon

FRIDAY
12th APRIL

morning

afternoon

**MOON ENTERS
GEMINI**
Toronto - 8.58am, London - 1.58pm
Sydney - 10.58pm

morning

afternoon

morning

afternoon

**MOON ENTERS
CANCER**

Toronto - 1.45pm, London - 6.45pm

**MOON ENTERS
CANCER**

Sydney - 3.45am

SUN IN TAURUS

Grounding Love & the Embodied Life

THE SECOND HOUSE - FIXED EARTH
PLANETARY RULER - VENUS

Toronto, London 19th April - 20th May
Sydney 20th April - 20th May

Fresh and reinvigorated from his journey through the dynamic starlands of Mars-ruled Aries, the Sun enters Taurus. A sigh of relief stretches across the lands as we collectively put our feet up and take a breath.
There is a lot to digest as we enter the Queendom of Venus.
Nature breathes in a complex series of rhythms, it takes some slowing down to observe and feel them. Current culture has hacked many of her secrets but we run a cropper when we ignore her. For she is us. We are nature, be it the rebellious child of the family.

We can stay awake till 3am scrolling, using up our endorphins on cat, makeup tutorials or gym-fail videos; or we can curl up with a body, be it one with skin or fur – block out the street lights, exile our phones and go to sleep early enough to wake with the Sun.

If we choose to do the latter, we connect to the primal circadian rhythms that Humans have evolved since the time of the great flood. Would your day improve if you got better quality sleep? Do you wake up feeling replenished and renewed with enough energy to thrive, not just to get by on?

Taurus reminds us that valuable treasures can be awakened through our body and that they've been created through divine wisdom as an expression of cosmic love.

All our bodies ask is that we love and care for them.
They are the vehicles we travel in, enabling our soul to experience all she
does, enfolding our spirit, granting us the opportunity to unfold our destiny
and to fulfil, on this extraordinary planet, what we've come to do.

Taurus season

CONSIDERATIONS

How are my sleep habits?
How might I love and care for my dear body more?
How often do I experience time in Nature?
How are my finances? Am I managing to save?

1st QUARTER MOON

Cancer

PUSHING THROUGH

15th April - Toronto 3.10am, London 8.10am
16th April - Sydney 3.10pm

As we move away from the powerful pull of the Solar Eclipse and, with Mercury still retrograde and conjunct Chiron, it's hard to get focused on what we need to do. Mars is sitting between Saturn and Neptune over in Pisces making it difficult to sustain motivation and will-force. Meanwhile the Cancerian Moon is asking us to check in with our feelings. How's your heart today?

WHAT WOULD IT TAKE TO HELP MODERATE YOUR 'FEELING' LIFE?

The week ahead

M

T

W

T

F

S

S

morning

afternoon

The weekly transits

First Quarter Moon in Cancer
Jupiter conjunct Uranus in Taurus
– Exact
Sun enters Taurus

1st QUARTER MOON
IN Cancer

Toronto - 3.11pm, London - 8.11pm

MOON ENTERS LEO

Toronto - 10.23pm

TUESDAY
16th APRIL

morning

afternoon

WEDNESDAY
17th APRIL

morning

afternoon

1st QUARTER MOON
IN *Cancer*
Sydney - 5.11am

MOON ENTERS LEO
London - 3.23am, Sydney - 12.23pm

THURSDAY
18th APRIL

morning

afternoon

**MOON ENTERS
VIRGO**

Toronto - 10.11am, London - 3.11pm

**JUPITER CONJUNCT
URANUS IN TAURUS**

Exact today through 26th April

FRIDAY
19th APRIL

morning

afternoon

**MOON ENTERS
VIRGO**

Sydney - 12.11am

SUN ENTERS TAURUS

Toronto - 10am, London - 3pm

SATURDAY
20th APRIL

morning

afternoon

SUNDAY
21st APRIL

morning

afternoon

SUN ENTERS TAURUS
Sydney - 12am

MOON ENTERS LIBRA
Toronto - 11.08pm

MOON ENTERS LIBRA
London - 4.08am, Sydney - 1.08 pm

FULL MOON

Scorpio

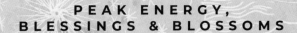

PEAK ENERGY,
BLESSINGS & BLOSSOMS

23rd April - Toronto 7.47pm
24th April - London 12.47am, Sydney 9.47am

The Taurean capacity for creating material wealth can inspire envy in those not so naturally gifted. It's easy to spot ostentatious wealth and, depending on our inclinations, we may either laugh at it or covet it. But it's not so funny when we realise that the bulk of the world's wealth is in the hands of relatively few. Most of us just want a home we love (one safe and secure), a car that runs well, and enough money to provide for our love ones – but that dream runs fast, and many of us spend most of our time and energy trying to catch it.

This secretive minority who hold all the cards, they're also the ones who feel the need to tell us how to live our lives. They've got a lot of 'good' plans for us that don't concern them.
It's a bit techy out there, with Pluto sitting at right angles between the Sun and Full Moon, all in fixed signs. Opinions may be running high.

WHAT IS YOUR EXPERIENCE
OF THIS FULL MOON?

....

....

....

....

Transits

MARS CONJUNCT NEPTUNE IN PISCES

23rd through 7th of May
Heightened Influence 26th April though 1st May

The song of the gulls tells Mars that land is near and he is about to step into his own as he prepares to glide into Aries. But until that happens, Neptune has zapped him and all he can manage is to put his feet up, drink rum and dream of siren songs.

MERCURY DIRECT IN ARIES

Conjunct the North Node 25th April
Leaves the Shadow Zone 14th May

There's no procrastinating or stationing for days. Mercury pivots direct on the North Node and slingshots, headstrong and future focused. He may be moving in a forwards motion, but until he passes the degree at which he turned retrograde, he is considered to be in the shadowlands.

The week ahead

M ....

T ....

W ....

T ....

F ....

S ....

S ....

morning

afternoon

The weekly transits

Full Moon in Scorpio
Mercury Direct in Aries
Mars conjunct Neptune in Pisces

TUESDAY
23rd APRIL

morning

afternoon

FULL MOON IN

Scorpio

Toronto - 7.47pm

WEDNESDAY
24th APRIL

morning

afternoon

FULL MOON IN

Scorpio

London - 12.47am, Sydney - 9.47 am

THURSDAY
25th APRIL

morning

afternoon

**MOON ENTERS
SAGITTARIUS**
Toronto - 9.37pm

**MERCURY DIRECT
IN ARIES**

FRIDAY
26th APRIL

morning

afternoon

**MOON ENTERS
SAGITTARIUS**
London - 2.37am, Sydney - 11.37am

**MARS CONJUNCT
NEPTUNE IN PISCES**
Heightened Influence today
through 1st May

SATURDAY
27th APRIL

morning

afternoon

SUNDAY
28th APRIL

morning

afternoon

MOON ENTERS CAPRICORN
Toronto - 5.37am,
London - 10.37am, Sydney - 7.37pm

VENUS

IN *Taurus*

Toronto, London, 29th April - 3rd May
Sydney 29th April - 4th May

THE MUSE

Venus works in the sphere of love, desire, creativity and relationships. She influences our personal magnetism, tastes and resources.

The moment Venus enters Taurus, she begins her journey to the far side of the Sun. Taurus is her natural abode, but her natural flow is coloured by her mission, and we will begin to experience her influence wane – more on this in a few weeks when we will explore her cycle in more detail.

LOVE AND DESIRE

Venus is calmly confident and at ease. She luxuriates in the pleasures of her senses and has an artist's touch in all her endeavours.

CREATIVITY AND INSPIRATION

To connect with Venus in Taurus, do what you love. This placement inspires us to live well, to create objects of beauty and utility... making our lives richer and more pleasurable.

THE MANNER OF RELATING

She is warm and her gentle manner touches all she meets. She doesn't push her point and she has patience in droves (until she doesn't).

Her generosity flows freely; she quietly understands that not everyone has her connection to abundance and how to manifest it. She's so stable and dependable... but don't be lulled into thinking that you are entitled to her – her presence is a gift. Don't disrespect the Goddess!

Warm and loving – Cold and indifferent
Consistent – Stubborn
Creative – Fixed

MARS

IN *Aries*

Toronto, London, Sydney 30th April - 8th June

THE WARRIOR

Mars works through our drives and desires; our ambitions and how we achieve them. He sets and secures our personal boundaries and defends us against those who transgress them.

DRIVES AND DESIRES

Mars is at home in Aries. Here, he's able to express his true nature unconstricted. He's ambitious, focused and competitive; he surpasses all expectations and crushes all obstacles in his way.

AMBITION AND WORK

Self motivated and up for any challenge, don't crowd him or try to micro manage, for he loves to work and needs no exterior prodding. Just keep feeding him with new and unusual challenges.

BOUNDARIES AND PROTECTION

If you struggle with boundary issues, note your impulses while Mars is in Aries; he'll school you in how to keep time wasters and succubus at bay – he's not a hater, he just knows what's his to deal with and what's not.

When Mars is in Aquarius you may experience: Vitality and endurance, self confidence, motivated and independent.

Difficulties you may encounter: Hard heads and stubborn hearts, overexertion.

3rd QUARTER MOON

Aquarius

REFLECT & RELEASE

1st May - Toronto 7.26am,
London 12.26pm, Sydney 9.26pm

The Moon passes by Pluto and themes that emerged during the Full Moon last week get a nudge along. With both Venus and Mars entering home turf and Mercury blasting direct, energy that's been blocked begins to flow. Go with it – it sure is nice not having to fight against the tide; however, keep in mind that we're heading into the rest-and-release phase of the Moon.

WHAT AREA OF MY LIFE AM I POWERING
THROUGH AT THE MOMENT?
WHAT AND WHERE AM I RELEASING?

Transits

MERCURY CONJUNCT CHIRON
– THIRD AND FINAL TIME IN 2024

27th April through 13th of May
Heightened Influence 4th through 10th May

Mercury sweeps past Chiron activating the themes that emerged around the 18th - 26th of March.
Can you place them? It may have to do with the young people in your life, or coming to a deeper understanding about aspects of your own inner child and the challenges you've faced. However this is playing out for you, Chiron is offering the key to a challenging riddle.

The week ahead

M

T

W

T

F

S

S

The weekly transits

Venus enters Taurus
Mars enters Aries
Third Quarter Moon in Aquarius
Mercury Direct conjunct Chiron in Aries

MONDAY
29th APRIL

morning

afternoon

VENUS ENTERS TAURUS

Toronto - 7.31am, London - 12.31pm,
Sydney - 9.31pm

TUESDAY
30th APRIL

morning

_____

_____

_____

_____

afternoon

_____

_____

_____

_____

_____

_____

MARS ENTERS ARIES
Toronto - 11.32am, London - 4.32pm

WEDNESDAY
1st MAY

morning

_____

_____

_____

_____

afternoon

_____

_____

_____

MARS ENTERS ARIES
Sydney 1.32am

3rd QUARTER MOON
in Aquarius
Toronto - 7.26am,
London - 12.26pm, Sydney - 9.26pm

THURSDAY
2nd MAY

morning

afternoon

FRIDAY
3rd MAY

morning

afternoon

MOON ENTERS PISCES
Toronto - 2.51pm, London - 7.51pm

MOON ENTERS PISCES
Sydney - 4.51am

SATURDAY
4th MAY

morning

afternoon

MOON ENTERS ARIES
Toronto - 4.40pm, London - 9.40pm

**MERCURY CONJUNCT
CHIRON IN ARIES**
Heightened Influence today
through 10th May

SUNDAY
5th MAY

morning

afternoon

MOON ENTERS ARIES
Sydney - 6.40am

NEW MOON
Taurus

PLANTING SEEDS

7th May - Toronto 10.21pm
8th May - London 4.21am, Sydney 1.21pm

It's darkest when the Sun and Moon meet; like a seed harnessing energy
to breakthrough the husk and burrow down roots, it's all happening
on the inside.
Jupiter and Uranus are pulsing out that signal of Ancient Earth magic
remembrance; Venus is stepping ever closer to the Sun in preparation
for her transformation. It's all happening in Taurus and that means
it's ours to implement and use.
We're supported to embody our beliefs. This is a slow process but Taurus
never plays the short game. It's a process involving patience, perseverance
and long-term gains made in incremental steps, with time allowed for rest
and play. We are invited to experience a practical, grounded alchemy where
we sculpt our soul through the act of completing our tasks.

*New Moon in Taurus themes: Embodying beliefs, feeling comfortable,
supported and nurtured. Finances and security.*

NEW MOON INTENTIONS

....

....

....

Transits

SUN CONJUNCT URANUS IN TAURUS

7th through 19th of May
Heightened Influence 10th through 16th May

Uranus shakes things up and the Sun shines his spotlight
on what and who has become stuck in the mud and fixed in their ways.
Prepare for some unsticking.

The week ahead

M

T

W

T

F

S

S

The weekly transits

New Moon in Taurus
Sun conjunct Uranus in Taurus

morning

afternoon

TUESDAY
7th MAY

morning

afternoon

NEW MOON IN
Taurus
Toronto - 10.21pm

WEDNESDAY
8th MAY

morning

afternoon

NEW MOON IN
Taurus
London - 4.21am, Sydney - 1.21pm

MOON ENTERS
GEMINI
Toronto - 7.20pm

THURSDAY
9th MAY

morning

afternoon

**MOON ENTERS
GEMINI**
London - 12.20am, Sydney - 9.20am

FRIDAY
10th MAY

morning

afternoon

**MOON ENTERS
CANCER**
Toronto - 11.13pm

**SUN CONJUNCT
URANUS IN TAURUS**
Heightened Influence today
through 16th May

SATURDAY
11th MAY

morning

afternoon

SUNDAY
12th MAY

morning

afternoon

MOON ENTERS
CANCER
London - 4.13am, Sydney - 1.13pm

1st QUARTER MOON

Leo

REFLECT & RELEASE

15th May - Toronto 7.47am,
London 12.47pm, Sydney 9.47pm

Leo colours the Moon's mood with playful bravado and gallantry, helping us push through obstacles with flair and loving humour. The Sun is conjunct Uranus – wait for the unexpected and if it doesn't show up – well, ride those high spirits and see where they take you!

HOW ARE YOUR NEW MOON INTENTIONS SHAPING UP?

_____

_____

_____

_____

_____

_____

_____

Transits

SUN CONJUNCT JUPITER IN TAURUS

12th through 25th of May
Heightened Influence 16th through 21st May

Bridging between Uranus to Jupiter, the Sun shines his light on the Jupiter/ Uranus conjunction that we explored on the 24th March. Have you observed any of the effects of this slow-moving transit?

When the Sun and Jupiter come together we can experience the profound satisfaction of understanding. It may come through the words of a teacher – or just drop into our heads and hearts as we're watching the birds. Savour it, for it is the nectar of the Gods.

The Venus Cycle

THE LONG JOURNEY
TO THE HEART OF THE SUN

The Morning Star retreats behind the Sun early May
Venus conjunct Sun – 2nd through 6th June
Venus emerges and reappears as the Evening Star in early July

Venus has gained speed and momentum and has begun her journey to the far side of the Sun. There, privately, in the light of our most radiant Star, she'll transform from the phosphorus maiden of the morning to the wise woman of the evening.

This transformation takes a few months and marks the midway point of her current cycle, which began in August of 2023.
(Do you recognise any patterns or recurring themes from that time?)
This cycle will conclude in March of 2025.

It can feel like our connection to love and inspiration is eclipsed when Venus ventures where we can't travel. As if we live in the memory of her gifts and have to learn to reconstruct them and fend for ourselves. We can feel bereft and unloved in the absence of her reassurance. Areas of life that we have assumed secure, may quake a little – watch for disruptions to finances and material wealth.

Remember what it is you value, even if you're not feeling it... She'll return nourished and renewed from her encounter with the Sun and we'll see her again as she calmly blazes across the evening sky.

WHERE ARE YOU BEING CHALLENGED?
WHAT DOES YOUR HEART YEARN FOR - OR WHOM?
WHAT ARE YOU ASKED TO RELEASE
AS YOU MATURE AND GROW?

The week ahead

M

T

W

T

F

S

S

The weekly transits

Mercury Leaves the Shadow Zone
First Quarter Moon in Leo
Venus continues her Cycle
Sun conjunct Jupiter in Taurus

MONDAY
13th MAY

morning

afternoon

MOON ENTERS LEO
Toronto - 7.20am,
London - 12.20am, Sydney - 9.20pm

TUESDAY
14th MAY

morning

afternoon

**MERCURY LEAVES
THE SHADOW ZONE**

WEDNESDAY
15th MAY

morning

afternoon

**1st QUARTER MOON
IN** *Leo*
Toronto - 7.47am,
London - 12.47pm, Sydney - 9.47pm

**MOON ENTERS
VIRGO**
Toronto - 5.33pm, London - 10.33pm

THURSDAY
16th MAY

morning

afternoon

**MOON ENTERS
VIRGO**
Sydney - 7.33am

**SUN CONJUNCT
JUPITER IN TAURUS**
Heightened Influence today
through 25th May

FRIDAY
17th MAY

morning

afternoon

SATURDAY
18th MAY

morning

afternoon

SUNDAY
19th MAY

morning

afternoon

MOON ENTERS LIBRA
Toronto - 6.23am, London - 11.23am,
Sydney - 8.23pm

SUN IN GEMINI

Connect & Communicate

THE THIRD HOUSE - MUTABLE AIR
PLANETARY RULER - MERCURY

Toronto and London 20th May - 20th June
Sydney 20th May - 21st June

Farewell the lush fields of Taurus as the Sun enters Mercury-ruled free flowing, breezy Gemini. Information, communication and movement are the life-force of this realm.

Mercury acts in the space in-between. He is the synapse to the neurone, deep in the labyrinthine brilliance of our brains. He is the electric charge of energy that liberates memories from locked cells; the bright force that opens floodgates for information and carves channels for new thoughts to flow. This electric synaptic charge is the life force of Gemini.

The Twins are always together, just as in life we are never alone. Look around, what do you see? I see a dog on the mat, Autumn crabapples outside the window, and I can hear the squawking of plovers in the distance. Wherever I am – there stands the other, constantly communicating their experiences of the world.

Gemini can speak as they are thinking, listen as they are talking; they can skim the surface like an airborne pebble skipping across a lake. With a lightness of touch and a gentle humour, they can lift us from the heaviness of emotional depths just when we're at risk of drowning.

There's an eternally-childlike curiosity at play in Gemini; an elegant dance of correspondence and courtesy. Interestingly, this enthusiasm for new ideas is what's recommended for our brain health. Language, music, mathematics, puzzles and problem solving all help to keep our synapses healthy and zapping, which in turn keeps our minds nimble and our memories accessible.

When we push through mental inertia and embrace learning we are saying 'yes' to the ever-youthful and carefree Gemini aspect of ourselves.

Gemini season

CONSIDERATIONS

How is my nervous system?
Am I feeling calm – or over stimulated? If so, how can
I regulate my nervous system?
What are my favourite conversations?
What am I doing for my brain health (puzzles, music, language, etc)?
Have my routines become sedentary?

FULL MOON

Sagittarius

PEAK ENERGY, BLESSINGS & BLOSSOMS

23rd May - Toronto 9.52am,
London 2.52pm, Sydney 11.52pm

Tonight's full Moon is a call to adventure and pulls us out of any small-minded concerns. Prepare for a massive incoming boost of Sagittarian insight, enthusiasm, warmth and a who-gives-a-nanny goat! Enjoy and let it flow.

Meanwhile Venus, still cloaked, is about to join the Sun in Gemini, but tonight she's standing by Jupiter on the final degree of Taurus. They're planning something wonderful, working together to give each of us something of great personal value. It may take a while to arrive, but if something wondrous drops in your lap over the next six weeks, say a little thank you to your celestial benefactors.

HOW HAVE YOUR NEW MOON INTENTIONS RIPENED?

....

....

....

....

....

VENUS

IN *Gemini*

Toronto 23rd May - 17th June
London, Sydney 24th May - 17th June

VENUS CONJUNCT THE SUN EXACT

2nd through 6th June

For the entire transit of Venus through Gemini she'll be obscured by the Sun and found in neither the evening nor the morning sky. It is a time to release – the course has been set and it is a time of ripening – even though her immediate influence is diminishing.

THE MUSE

Venus works in the sphere of love, desire, creativity and relationships. She influences our personal magnetism, tastes and resources.

LOVE AND DESIRE

Venus is Gemini adores exploring the multitude of possibilities that offer. It's not that she doesn't want stability, but how to choose when there are so many fascinating options? How to commit to just one...

CREATIVITY AND INSPIRATION

To connect with Venus in Gemini allow your mind to expand and be open to all manner of communications and experiences. Her talents are manifold and she's inspired by engaging with new people, social circles, ideas and new approaches to old dilemmas.

THE MANNER OF RELATING

She is light of touch and subtlety nuanced; a skilful communicator who can spin a yarn with threads whose themes are chosen from across the ages. She'll weave you a tapestry rich in colour, understanding and wit. If you're down in the dumps she'll create a bridge, spun of light and words, for you to cross into a delightfully-intelligent and beautiful world.

Understanding – Moves on quickly
Curious – Superficial
Focused – Scattered

JUPITER

IN *Gemini*

THE TRAVELLING PHILOSOPHER
- A YEAR LONG TRANSIT
26th May 2024 through 10th June 2025

Jupiter is the planet of plenty. His energy is expansive, wise and fair. Under his tutelage we are driven to seek higher knowledge and wisdom.

Jupiter amplifies as he shifts from rich-earthy Taurus wisdom into the accelerated, high-frequency domains of Gemini. Here, he charms writers, podcasters, teachers and poets, coders and technology-and-delivery-driven businesses. His touch will be felt as we communicate, travel and connect with each other: his charms especially favour broadminded attitudes and versatile minds.

Jupiter travels around our Sun every 12 years, and once a year he changes sign, heralding transformation in a new sector of our lives. In astrology, Jupiter's influence is considered fortuitous; he expands, like a growth agent, upon what's already there.

I invite you to investigate this by exploring your experiences of the previous times that Jupiter has travelled through Gemini. As memories emerge, you'll begin to find themes which will, in turn, indicate the nature of the shifts coming your way over the course of the 12 months.

June 2012 - June 2013
April 1976 - August 1977
June 2000 - June 2001
April 1965 - May 1966
July 1988 - July 1989
May 1953 - May 1954

WHAT BIG SHIFTS OCCURRED FOR YOU DURING THE
YEARS THAT JUPITER WAS IN GEMINI AND WHAT
WHERE THE TAKE-AWAY LESSONS?

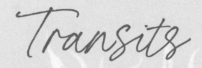

Transits

SUN IN GEMINI TRINE PLUTO IN AQUARIUS

19th through 26th of June
Heightened Influence 22nd through 24th May

Trines are a supportive transit, but mission-driven Pluto is always prodding and poking. I wonder who or what will be turned upside down and revealed? Where will the Gemini Sun, with his bright intelligence and quick wits, focus his light?

VENUS IN GEMINI TRINE PLUTO IN AQUARIUS

22nd through 28th of May
Heightened Influence 24th through 26th May

There's powerful chemistry afoot when Venus and Pluto meet. However, it is a highly unstable energy and can turn toxic even when you really, really don't want it to ... Hearts are already tender with Venus's long hiatus – be wise around overly-compelling invitations and scenarios.

JUPITER IN GEMINI TRINE PLUTO IN AQUARIUS

The Philosopher and the Technocrats

18th May through 19th June 2025
Heightened Influence 26th May through 7th June

Culture and Society – Pluto's been finding his footing since entering Aquarius in January. Make way, make way! Jupiter's coming to *supercharge* his agenda – it's not dissimilar to a start up that just got capital. Pluto doesn't just get free reign, Jupiter brings his sense of fairplay, honour and wisdom... Will Pluto listen, or simply dig in his heels, nod in agreement (whilst solidifying his position), and then snatch the money and run?

Individual – This transit will empower us to be bolder than we usually are. Think grandiose – like being caught in a fever dream where the volume keeps rising and no one can hear because of the collective cacophony. There's momentum for hustling projects forwards, but check that any deals struck during this period are fair and equitable.

The analytical depths of Pluto, combined with the expansive wisdom of Jupiter, make this a powerful time for meditative and inner spiritual work.

The week ahead

M

T

W

T

F

S

S

The weekly transits

Sun enters Gemini
Jupiter enters Gemini
Full Moon in Sagittarius
Jupiter in Gemini trine Pluto in Aquarius
Venus enters Gemini
Venus in Gemini trine Pluto in Aquarius

MONDAY
20th MAY

morning

afternoon

SUN ENTERS GEMINI
Toronto - 8.59am, London - 1.59pm,
Sydney - 10.59pm

MOON ENTERS SCORPIO
Toronto - 11.34pm, London - 6.34pm

TUESDAY
21st MAY

morning

_____
_____
_____
_____
_____

afternoon

_____
_____
_____
_____
_____
_____

MOON ENTERS SCORPIO
Sydney - 8.34am

WEDNESDAY
22nd MAY

morning

_____
_____
_____
_____
_____

afternoon

_____
_____
_____
_____
_____
_____

SUN IN GEMINI TRINE PLUTO IN AQUARIUS
Today through 24th

THURSDAY
23rd MAY

morning

....

....

....

....

....

afternoon

....

....

....

....

FRIDAY
24th MAY

morning

....

....

....

....

....

afternoon

....

....

....

....

FULL MOON IN
Sagittarius
Toronto - 9.52am, London - 2.52pm,
Sydney - 11.52pm

VENUS ENTERS GEMINI
Toronto - 4.30pm, London - 9.30pm

VENUS ENTERS GEMINI
Sydney - 6.30am

VENUS IN GEMINI TRINE PLUTO IN AQUARIUS
Today through 26th May

SATURDAY
25th MAY

morning

afternoon

**MOON ENTERS
CAPRICORN**
Toronto - 11.35am, London - 4.35pm

SUNDAY
26th MAY

morning

afternoon

**MOON ENTERS
CAPRICORN**
Sydney - 1.35am
**PLUTO ENTERS
GEMINI**

**JUPITER IN GEMINI
TRINE PLUTO IN
AQUARIUS**
Today through 7th June

3rd QUARTER MOON

Pisces

REFLECT & RELEASE

30th May - Toronto 1.10pm, London 6.10pm
31st May - Sydney 3.10am

With Mars conjunct Chiron, and Venus still enmeshed with the Sun, you may be feeling a little wan and washed out. The Pisces Moon encourages us to follow the path of least resistance – pick whatever low-hanging fruit may have ripened since the Full Moon.

PUT YOUR FEET UP AND REVIEW:
WHAT REALLY NEEDS DOING AND
WHAT CAN I LET SLIP FOR THE TIME BEING?

Transits

MARS CONJUNCT CHIRON IN ARIES

22nd May through 8th of June
Heightened Influence 27th May through 3rd June

Mars is all action and momentum, and we experience this influence through our will-force, our capacity to become motivated, and our ability to see things through. When he comes into aspect with Chiron we can feel deflated. Energy levels may run low. If you're tired, rest. If there's a lot being asked of you that you really can't put on hold, pace yourself, stay hydrated and well nourished.

MERCURY CONJUNCT URANUS IN TAURUS

29th through 4th of June
Heightened Influence 31st through 2nd June

As the Sun travels through Gemini and through a realm of fantastic ideas, Mercury comes flying past Uranus in Taurus – dropping some info that reminds us that adjustments are an option and that we're far more flexible than we sometimes give ourselves credit for.

The week ahead

M

T

W

T

F

S

S

The weekly transits

Mars conjunct Chiron in Aries
Third Quarter Moon in Pisces
Mercury conjunct Uranus in Taurus
Venus conjunct Sun exact

MONDAY
27th MAY

morning

afternoon

MOON ENTERS AQUARIUS
Toronto - 4.45pm, London - 9.45pm

MARS CONJUNCT CHIRON IN ARIES
Today through 3rd June

TUESDAY
28th MAY

morning

afternoon

WEDNESDAY
29th MAY

morning

afternoon

MOON ENTERS
AQUARIUS
Sydney - 6.45am

THURSDAY
30th MAY

morning

afternoon

3rd QUARTER MOON

IN *Pisces*

Toronto - 1.10pm, London - 6.10pm

FRIDAY
31st MAY

morning

afternoon

3rd QUARTER MOON

IN *Pisces*

Sydney - 3.10am

MERCURY CONJUNCT
URANUS IN TAURUS

Today through 2nd June

MOON ENTERS ARIES

Toronto - 11.28pm

SATURDAY
1st JUNE

morning

afternoon

SUNDAY
2nd JUNE

morning

afternoon

MOON ENTERS ARIES
London - 4.28am, Sydney - 1.28pm

VENUS CONJUNCT SUN
Today through 6th June

NEW MOON

Gemini

CONJUNCT VENUS

PLANTING SEEDS

6th June Toronto 8.36am,
London 1.36pm, Sydney 10.36pm

When the Sun and Moon meet, the sky is at its darkest and the void is humming with the potential of the New Moon's cycle. There's information that wants to be known. I can't tell you the delivery system, but it's likely to be about the past, with just enough goodness to give you a sense that the future holds a taste of sweetness. The revelation or conversation may be tender and close to our hearts. It's a perfect New Moon for journal work.

Saturn in Pisces is forming a hard square to the Sun, Moon and Venus, indicating that there's a build up of pressure – possibly from an older friend or family member. As the situation plays out, remember that you can't walk in two directions at once. Something has to give.

New Moon in Gemini themes: Receiving and transmitting messages, meaningful communication, journalling and planing

NEW MOON INTENTIONS

Transits

MERCURY CONJUNCT JUPITER IN GEMINI TRINE PLUTO IN AQUARIUS

1st through 6th of June
Heightened Influence 3rd through 5th June

This is the perfect window for scheduling important meetings. Mercury's at home and confident. He's synced into Jupiter's expansive and philosophical tendencies, whilst channeling Pluto's power via a supportive trine from intellectually-minded Aquarius. Name the conversation you'd like to have?

MERCURY

IN *Pisces*

4th June – 2nd July Toronto, London, Sydney

THE MESSENGER

Mercury influences how we transmit and receive information, our ideas and conversations as well as influencing movement, trade and travel.

Mercury in Gemini is quick on his toes and even faster in thought. Information gets stored in real time and he processes facts and tidbits in multiple categories – ordered according to the potential need to speedily retrieve them, for insertion into conversations.

When under helpful influences, he is charming, refreshingly youthful, insightful and curious; he knows that each side of a story has merit and wants a glimpse from every perspective. This can get him into trouble. Some signs feel that is a breach of ethics and personal trust, but he achieves a sense of wholeness, one snippet of info at a time. If one piece is missing, the puzzle will never be solved. His highly-charged, electric mind is a racehorse that some of us can ride gleefully . For others, or indeed ourselves at other times, there may be a need to get off and find a quiet, safe, dim room to settle the senses.

It is a brilliant time for learning, teaching, presentations and communication.

Sharp and quick witted – Scattered
A wide range of interests – Superficial knowledge
Open minded – Impressionable

I'VE BEEN THINKING ABOUT… I JUST WANT TO SAY…

MARS
in *Taurus*

Toronto, London 30th April - 20th July
Sydney 1st May - 21st July

THE WARRIOR

Mars works through our drives and desires; our ambitions and how we achieve them. He sets and secures our personal boundaries and defends us against those who transgress them.

DRIVES AND DESIRES

Mars in Taurus derives a lot of satisfaction from the creature comforts. Think artisan and organic food, fine wine, a sensuous partner and great art; think a safe stashed with gold bullion and cash, with space enough for next week's savings to be added.

AMBITION AND WORK

He may be slow to start, but once he sets course he will invest long hours over many years, working patiently and diligently to get the outcome he desires. He wants the good life and that doesn't mean going low grade until he gets there.

BOUNDARIES AND PROTECTION

Having money and being financially secure acts as security against the shifting sands of fate. Mars will build a fortress to keep kin and clan safe. He's slow to anger, but if the bullies keep nipping his ankles (or those of any in said clan) he has the strength and endurance to bulldoze those foolish antagonists.

When Mars is in Taurus you may experience: Endurance, staying power, patience and a capacity for hard work and big projects.

Difficulties you may encounter: Inflexibility, inertia, getting stuck in the mud of life (difficulty getting free of old patterns and relationships).

INTENTIONS, INSIGHTS & REFLECTIONS

The week ahead

M
_____

T
_____

W
_____

T
_____

F
_____

S
_____

S
_____

The weekly transits

Mercury enters Gemini
Mercury conjunct Jupiter in Gemini
trine Pluto in Aquarius
New Moon in Gemini
Mars enters Taurus

morning

afternoon

MOON ENTERS TAURUS
Toronto - 12.55am, London - 5.55am,
Sydney - 3.55pm

MERCURY CONJUNCT JUPITER IN GEMINI TRINE PLUTO IN AQUARIUS
Today through 5th June

TUESDAY
4th JUNE

morning

afternoon

WEDNESDAY
5th JUNE

morning

afternoon

MERCURY ENTERS GEMINI
Toronto - 1.56am, London - 6.56am,
Sydney - 3.56pm

MOON ENTERS GEMINI
Toronto - 4.36am, London - 9.36am,
Sydney - 6.36pm

THURSDAY
6th JUNE

morning

afternoon

NEW MOON IN
Gemini
Toronto - 8.36am, London - 1.36pm,
Sydney - 10.36pm

FRIDAY
7th JUNE

morning

afternoon

MOON ENTERS CANCER
Toronto - 8.41am, London - 1.41pm,
Sydney - 10.41pm

SATURDAY
8th JUNE

morning

afternoon

SUNDAY
9th JUNE

morning

afternoon

MARS ENTERS TAURUS
Toronto - 12.35am, London - 5.35am,
Sydney - 2.35pm

MOON ENTERS LEO
Toronto - 3.28pm

1st QUARTER MOON
Virgo

MOMENTUM & GROWTH

14th June - Toronto 1.15am,
London 6.15am, Sydney 3.15pm

If you are feeling a yen to get stuff sorted – that'd be the Virgo Moon.
It appears there's a lot to be said. Mercury is cloaked by the Sun and if the
words you're speaking aren't streaming out and being received the way you
intend them to be, give it a few days. Mercury will meet up with Venus and
there's a soothing message to be received. Remember we are moving into
that release and restore phase of the Moon.

WHAT HAVE I ACHIEVED
AND WHAT DO I NEED TO RELEASE?

_____

_____

_____

_____

_____

_____

_____

Transits

MERCURY, SUN AND VENUS CONJUNCT IN GEMINI (AND INTO CANCER TOGETHER)

11th through 4th of June
Heightened Influence 13th through 21st June

Mercury wants to know what's been going on, with whom, when and where. The Sun – always shedding light – has nothing to hide. Venus is accelerating and beginning to separate from the Sun. This makes for interesting conversations down on earth amongst us humans. It's personal. Someone may need a little space. The trio enter Cancer together, indicating that no matter how wordsy things get, an emotionally-satisfying solution will be reached.

The week ahead

M
....

T
....

W
....

T
....

F
....

S
....

S
....

The weekly transits

Mercury, Sun and Venus conjunct in
Gemini (then into Cancer together)
First Quarter Moon in Virgo

morning
....
....
....
....

afternoon
....
....
....
....
....
....
....

MOON ENTERS LEO
London - 8.28pm, Sydney - 5.28am

TUESDAY
11th JUNE

morning

afternoon

WEDNESDAY
12th JUNE

morning

afternoon

MERCURY, SUN & VENUS CONJUNCT IN GEMINI (THEN INTO CANCER TOGETHER)
Today through 21st June

MOON ENTERS VIRGO
Toronto - 1.38am, London - 6.38am, Sydney - 3.38pm

THURSDAY
13th JUNE

morning

afternoon

FRIDAY
14th JUNE

morning

afternoon

3rd QUARTER MOON
IN *Virgo*
Toronto - 1.15am, London - 6.15am,
Sydney - 3.15pm

MOON ENTERS LIBRA
Toronto - 2.12pm, London - 7.12pm

morning

morning

afternoon

afternoon

MOON ENTERS LIBRA
Sydney - 4.12am

SUN IN CANCER

The Many Faces of Feelings

THE FOURTH HOUSE - CARDINAL WATER
PLANETARY RULER - MOON

Toronto & London 20th June - 22nd July
Sydney 21st June - 22nd July

Entering the Moon's domain the Sun steps into Cancer and we enter the mysterious realm of feelings. The symbol of Cancer is the the crab and the first thing we notice, aside from those big nippers, is her exoskeleton. This is the hard outer shell that protects her soft inner self from the external environment.

Likewise the Cancerian element of ourselves needs a barrier to protect our internal world from the harshness of exposure. We need to allow time and space to process the complex and ever-shifting tides of the emotional realms.

Our house can be seen as a type of exoskeleton; as a thick, brick and mortar skin that protect us. Our home is our safe place where we can unfold private experiences and observe the exterior world through windows and behind screens. Tucked in safely like a crustacean in a seaside cave.

This doesn't mean we spend all Cancer Season bunkered down, getting all moody, broody and dwelling on everything that's ever happened to us. Rather, as we are processing the complex inter relational dynamics of those around us, we are scoping the horizon for the best time to scuttle into the fray and make our play.

It takes maturity of soul to move through the multitude of emotional states that can unfold in a day and wisdom to process emotions in real time. For many of us, it takes courage to reveal the tender feelings of our inner beings, but how lonely would life be if we never did?

Cancer season
CONSIDERATIONS

Do I process my emotions in real time, or am I prone to sit on my feelings?
How am I at expressing my emotions?
Do I neglect my own emotional health for the sake of not making a scene?
Am I clinging to ancient hurts at the expense of my current happiness?
If so, how might I release them?

VENUS

IN *Cancer*

Toronto, London & Sydney 17th June - 11th July

THE MUSE

Venus works in the sphere of love, desire, creativity and relationships. She influences our personal magnetism, tastes and resources.

LOVE AND DESIRE

Venus in the realm of the Moon is ultra feminine – she's emotionally attuned, highly sensitive and intuitive. Her gifts unfold once she feels safe and secure; however, until then it can be a roller coaster of emotions as her tender heart seeks out true love.

CREATIVITY AND INSPIRATION

Highly imaginative, she's seldom stuck for inspiration. Her fertile mind can read an entire story in passing clouds and your destiny in the tea leaves.

THE MANNER OF RELATING

Vanus in Cancer is deeply interested in your feelings and she knows how to soothe the aching places. Once she's found love, be it romantic, platonic or familial, she is faithful and loyal to a fault. She will expect the same – please, help her battle the demon of her insecurity, and let her know how wonderful she is.

Warm and loving – Clinging and too attached
Wise and understanding – Easily hurt
Creative – Shy and insecure

I'M SO INSPIRED BY… I LOVE…
IT DRIVES ME CRAZY WHEN…
EXPLORE WHEN THE MOOD STRIKES

FULL MOON

Capricorn

PEAK ENERGY, BLESSINGS & BLOSSOMS

21st June - Toronto 8.07pm,
London 1.07am, Sydney 11.07am

It's time for those zooming thoughts to land. We are in the realm of feelings now. Have you noticed a shift this week?

The Moon, practical, serene and queenly in Capricorn helps us anchor as we acclimatise to the emotional richness of this Cancer Season. Survey your domain and enjoy what you have created.

HOW HAVE INTENTIONS MADE ON THE NEW MOON MANIFESTED?

_____

_____

_____

_____

_____

_____

MERCURY

IN *Cancer*

Toronto, London & Sydney 17th June - 2nd July

THE MESSENGER

Mercury influences how we transmit and receive information, our ideas and conversations as well as influencing movement, trade and travel.

Mercury enters Cancer and a vast historical landscape of events and stashed emotions open up. His quick wits size up interpersonal dynamics and conversations take an intimate tone. Memories reappear from the depths as new understanding emerges.

He holds counsel to many, lending his inquisitive ear, making them feel seen and heard. He can recall everything ever confided to him and his advice is measured and carefully analysed.

An avid historian, he'll detect missing links, find new doors and may retell old, near forgotten stories with emotional nuance and humour.

Mercury in Cancer thrives on the deeper questions. He helps us to process our emotions in real time and to turn experiences into life wisdom, which can then be drawn on as needed.

Emotional Insight – Moody and secretive
Strong memory – May take offence when challenged
An empathic listener – Will remember every perceived slight

The week ahead

M

T

W

T

F

S

S

The weekly transits

Venus enters Cancer
Mercury enters Cancer
Sun enters Cancer
Full Moon in Capricorn

morning

afternoon

MOON ENTERS SCORPIO
Toronto - 1.37am, London - 6.37am,
Sydney - 4.37pm

VENUS ENTERS CANCER
Toronto - 1.20am, London - 6.20am,
Sydney - 4.20pm

MERCURY ENTERS CANCER
Toronto - 4.06am, London - 9.06am,
Sydney - 7.06pm

TUESDAY
18th JUNE

morning

afternoon

WEDNESDAY
19th JUNE

morning

afternoon

**MOON ENTERS
SAGITTARIUS**
Toronto - 11.32pm, London - 4.32pm

THURSDAY
20th JUNE

morning

afternoon

MOON ENTERS SAGITTARIUS
Sydney - 2.32am

SUN ENTERS CANCER
Toronto - 4.32pm, London - 9.32pm

FRIDAY
21st JUNE

morning

afternoon

SUN ENTERS CANCER
Sydney - 7.32 am

FULL MOON IN
Capricorn
Toronto - 8.07pm

SATURDAY
22nd JUNE

morning

afternoon

FULL MOON IN

Capricorn

London - 1.07am, Sydney - 11.07am

SUNDAY
23rd JUNE

morning

afternoon

MOON ENTERS
AQUARIUS

Toronto - 10.14pm

3rd QUARTER MOON

Aries

REFLECT & RELEASE

28th June - Toronto 4.54pm, London 9.54pm
29th June - Sydney 7.54am

Tonight, there's no lullaby being sung by the Aries' Moon.

I hear some spluttering and possibly expletives as we push on through. You are supported with what you need to do, to get where you need to be. Afterwards, as the Moon winds up this cycle, leaving us depleted and the sky dark, rest well, knowing you've done all you could.

WHAT HAVE I ACHIEVED
AND WHAT DO I NEED TO RELEASE?

Transits

MERCURY IN CANCER TRINE SATURN IN PISCES

24th through 29th of June
Heightened Influence 26th through 28th June

As we wade into deeper water, questions around maturity and emotional responsibility arise. We are invited to swim into depths with one another. If you're encountering a touch of melancholy, accept the invitation to feel and explore what is being communicated.

The week ahead

M

T

W

T

F

S

S

The weekly transits

Mercury in Cancer
trine Saturn in Pisces
Third Quarter Moon in Aries

morning

afternoon

**MOON ENTERS
AQUARIUS**
London - 3.14am, Sydney - 1.14pm

TUESDAY
25th JUNE

morning

afternoon

WEDNESDAY
26th JUNE

morning

afternoon

MERCURY IN CANCER TRINE SATURN IN PISCES
Today through 28th June

MOON ENTERS PISCES
Toronto - 1.08am, London - 6.08am, Sydney - 4.08pm

THURSDAY
27th JUNE

morning

afternoon

FRIDAY
28th JUNE

morning

afternoon

3rd QUARTER MOON
IN *Aries*
Toronto - 4.54pm, London - 9.54pm

SATURDAY
29th JUNE

morning

afternoon

SUNDAY
30th JUNE

morning

afternoon

MERCURY

IN *Leo*

Toronto, London 2nd July – 25th July
Sydney 2nd July – 26th July

THE MESSENGER

Mercury influences how we transmit and receive information, our ideas and conversations as well as influencing movement, trade and travel.

Mercury in Leo knows just what to say and he'll say it with confidence, even if the facts don't completely back him up. You'll forgive him as he tells the tale with such gusto and drama. The brush strokes may be broad, but ALL the colours are there, and you'll feel like you've lived through the events described. He's up for public speaking, also to speaking for an audience of one, but when there's no one to listen, it's a dejected sight. That deflated little lion in a box, that's him. But not for long. Soon a narrative starts bouncing around his brain, he's working up a new tale and it's entertaining him, so, by the logic of it, it'll entertain you as well.

He particularly values appreciation so pointing out his factual errors too often, may leave you out of the orb of his warm enthusiasm. It may look like he's all confidence and perpetually performance ready, but the price he pays can be some tricky egotism. It stings him, more than it hurts you. Perhaps, in those self-absorbed moments he forgets that it's not all about him and that he's the vessel for divine inspiration to flow through.

It's a brilliant time for public speaking, story telling, writing, drama classes, teaching and presentations.

Brilliant storyteller – Forgets the facts
Natural leaders – Bossy
Speaks from the heart – Self important

I'VE BEEN THINKING ABOUT...
I JUST WANT TO SAY...

NEW MOON

Cancer

PLANTING SEEDS

5th July - Toronto 5.56pm, London 10.56am
6th June - Sydney 8.56am

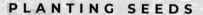

When the Moon is in Cancer she is at her most relaxed, generous and nourishing. It's like stepping through the door after a long trip. Familiar smells and sounds greet you. It's your kitchen and your bathroom and most importantly your very own, just-right-for-you bed. You are home and you are safe.

This new Moon is perfect for intentions around what you need to feel safe, nurtured and nourished. You give so much to those around you, but without the anchor of self care, is it sustainable?

New Moon in Cancer themes: Emotional harmony, deep intuition, family ties and relationships, home.

NEW MOON INTENTIONS

Transits

MERCURY IN CANCER TRINE NEPTUNE IN PISCES WITH A TOUCH OF URANUS IN TAURUS

29th June through 5th July
Heightened Influence 1st through 3rd July

Super fanciful, new and unbelievably-magical ideas are beaming down our way for a few short days. Logic may have no place here whatsoever. Or, that solution you never could quite find may spring from the most unlikely of sources. Enjoy!

VENUS IN CANCER TRINE SATURN IN PISCES

29th June through 6th July
Heightened Influence 2nd through 4th July

Venus is preparing to take her place in the evening sky. She greets Saturn in Pisces with a nod of recognition; her journey has been so long. Growing up is a process of initiations which change you irrevocably, one experience at a time. She smiles in appreciation for the wisdom gained.

The week ahead

M

T

W

T

F

S

S

morning

afternoon

The weekly transits

Mercury enters Leo
Venus in Cancer trine Saturn in Pisces
New Moon in Cancer

MERCURY IN CANCER TRINE NEPTUNE IN PISCES WITH A TOUCH OF URANUS IN TAURUS

Today through 3rd July

TUESDAY
2nd JULY

morning

afternoon

MERCURY ENTERS LEO
Toronto - 7.50am, London - 12.50pm, Sydney - 10.50pm

VENUS IN CANCER TRINE SATURN IN PISCES
Today through 4th July

WEDNESDAY
3rd JULY

morning

afternoon

MOON ENTERS GEMINI
Toronto - 8.50pm, London - 1.50am, Sydney - 11.50am

THURSDAY
4th JULY

morning

afternoon

FRIDAY
5th JULY

morning

afternoon

**MOON ENTERS
CANCER**
Sydney - 6.51am

**MOON ENTERS
CANCER**
Toronto - 8.51pm, London - 3.51pm

NEW MOON IN *Cancer*
Toronto - 5.56pm, London - 10.56am

SATURDAY
6th JULY

morning

afternoon

NEW MOON IN *Cancer*
Sydney - 8.56am

MOON ENTERS LEO
Toronto - 10.56 pm, London - 3.56 am

SUNDAY
7th JULY

morning

afternoon

MOON ENTERS LEO
Sydney - 1.56 pm

VENUS

IN *Leo*

Toronto, London & Sydney 11th July - 5th August

THE MUSE

Venus works in the sphere of love, desire, creativity and relationships. She influences our personal magnetism, tastes and resources.

LOVE AND DESIRE

Venus in Leo loves LOVE. She'll adore you and she flourishes under acts of generosity and open displays of affection. Withholding affection from her is like depriving a plant of sunshine.

CREATIVITY AND INSPIRATION

To connect with Venus in Leo open your heart. What makes you happiest? Her energy is infectious and she'll help you find an audience for your talents. If you are of a shy and introspective nature this may sound less then inviting, but it's all to a scale. Which area of your life will you ask her to amplify?

THE MANNER OF RELATING

She is enthusiastic and warm. Emotions are declared and you won't be confused where you stand with her. In turn, she needs to know exactly what she means to you. Emotional ambiguity is one of her worst nightmares and the other is being caught in a secretive scenario where she has to withhold heralding her passion and love to the world. Now's the time to speak directly from the heart.

Warm and loving – Easily offended
Loyal – Conditional
Creative – Insecure

I'M SO INSPIRED BY... I LOVE...
IT DRIVES ME CRAZY WHEN...
EXPLORE WHEN THE MOOD STRIKES

1st QUARTER MOON

Libra

PUSHING THROUGH

13th July - Toronto 11.47pm, London 6.47pm
14th July - Sydney 8.47am

In Libra, the Moon is gentle with a sweet unassuming air. Tonight, she stands opposite Chiron. He has a wounded expression on his face and the question of 'Why?' hangs between them.

WHAT IS IT THAT NEEDS CLEARING AND REBALANCING AS YOU PROGRESS WITH YOUR NEW MOON INTENTIONS?

Transits

VENUS IN CANCER THEN INTO LEO TRINE NEPTUNE IN PISCES

8th through 14th July
Heightened Influence 10th through 13th July

At last! Venus emerges and she receives a loving beam from Neptune in Pisces. It's an invitation to celebrate, to let go and flow into the dream of union and togetherness. With Uranus throwing in a fistfull of sparks from Taurus, it could go over the top. But Venus is the calm Queen here; she can participate without losing her head.

SUN IN CANCER SQUARE CHIRON IN ARIES

10th through 20th of July
Heightened Influence 14th through 17th July

Has your anger been diluted into a sea of small, groggy emotions? The Sun dries out the mud flats and it's a salty harvest. Themes from the New Moon in April return. Can you detect the story?

MARS CONJUNCT URANUS IN TAURUS

10th through 21st July
Heightened Influence 14th through 19th July

You are granted cosmic permission to push through stubborn blocks. This is the sledge-hammer demolition phase of the renovations – messy but necessary.

The week ahead

M
....

T
....

W
....

T
....

F
....

S
....

S
....

The weekly transits

Venus in Cancer then into Leo trine
Neptune in Pisces
Venus enters Leo
First Quarter Moon in Libra
Sun in Cancer square Chiron in Aries
Mars conjunct Uranus in Taurus

morning

afternoon

TUESDAY
9th JULY

morning

afternoon

WEDNESDAY
10th JULY

morning

afternoon

**MOON ENTERS
VIRGO**
Toronto - 9.47am, London - 2.47pm,
Sydney - 11.47pm

**VENUS IN CANCER
THEN INTO LEO
TRINE NEPTUNE IN
PISCES**
Today through 13th July

THURSDAY
11th JULY

morning

afternoon

MOON ENTERS LIBRA
Toronto - 10.06pm

VENUS ENTERS LEO
Toronto - 12.18pm, London - 5.18pm

FRIDAY
12th JULY

morning

afternoon

MOON ENTERS LIBRA
London - 3.06am, Sydney - 12.06pm

VENUS ENTERS LEO
Sydney - 12.18am

SATURDAY
13th JULY

morning

afternoon

1st QUARTER MOON
IN *Libra*
Toronto - 11.47pm, London - 6.47pm

SUNDAY
14th JULY

morning

afternoon

1st QUARTER MOON
IN *Libra*
Sydney - 8.47am

MOON ENTERS SCORPIO
Toronto - 10.53am, London - 3.53pm

SUN IN CANCER SQUARE CHIRON IN ARIES
Today through 17th June

MARS CONJUNCT URANUS IN TAURUS
Today through 21st Jun

MARS

IN *Gemini*

Toronto, London 20th July - 4th September
Sydney 21st July - 3rd September

THE WARRIOR

Mars works through our drives and desires; our ambitions and how we achieve them. He sets and secures our personal boundaries and defends us against those who transgress them.

DRIVES AND DESIRES

Playful and with restless energy, it's not difficult to catch his attention. It may be a challenge to hold it. He wants ALL the experiences... at least once.

AMBITION AND WORK

Boredom is the life-sucking enemy of Mars in Gemini. His attention span and focus may flit, but so long as there are interesting options he's a powerhouse of productivity. His will-force will fade the moment his interest does.

BOUNDARIES AND PROTECTION

Words can become weapons for Mars in Gemini. His sharp wit can tear down an opponent and he can debate his adversary into a state of confusion and fatigue.

When Mars is in Gemini you may experience: Heightened mobility, a capacity for multitasking, adaptability.

Difficulties you may encounter: Scattered focus, difficulty committing, restlessness and difficulty seeing projects through.

FULL MOON

Capricorn

PEAK ENERGY, BLESSINGS & BLOSSOMS

21st July - Toronto 6.16am,
London 11.16am, Sydney 8.16pm

The last Full Moon was in the early degrees of Capricorn and tonight her brightness shines through the final degree.
Her close proximity to Pluto speaks of emotional pressure and a perilous path. But we can be confident that we won't slip and lose our serene crown. The Capricorn Moon is a born survivor – as are we, and that is worth a quiet and possibly emotionally-reserved celebration.

HOW HAVE INTENTIONS MADE ON THE NEW MOON MANIFESTED?

....

....

....

....

....

....

Transits

SUN IN CANCER TRINE NEPTUNE IN PISCES

18th through 26th July
Heightened Influence 21st through 23rd July

Happiness flows like water around a sea otter's rolling body. Sweetness and daydreams splash, with rainbows born through sunshine and droplets.

SUN IN CANCER THEN LEO
OPPOSITE PLUTO IN AQUARIUS

18th through 27th of July
Heightened Influence 21st through 25th July

Whoever, whatever you're facing off against may exert pressure. But once your emotions settle you'll see that nobody carries the light you do and that your shine is non-negotiable.

The week ahead

M

T

W

T

F

S

S

The weekly transits

Full Moon in Capricorn
Mars enters Gemini
Sun in Cancer trine Neptune in Pisces
Sun in Cancer then
Leo opposite Pluto in Aquarius

morning

afternoon

MOON ENTERS SCORPIO
Sydney - 12.53am

TUESDAY
16th JULY

morning

afternoon

**MOON ENTERS
SAGITTARIUS**
Toronto - 9.25pm

WEDNESDAY
17th JULY

morning

afternoon

**MOON ENTERS
SAGITTARIUS**
London - 2.25am, Sydney - 11.25am

THURSDAY
18th JULY

morning

afternoon

FRIDAY
19th JULY

morning

afternoon

MOON ENTERS
CAPRICORN
Toronto - 6.16am, London - 11.16am,
Sydney - 8.16pm

SATURDAY
20th JULY

morning

afternoon

MARS ENTERS GEMINI
Toronto - 4.43am, London - 9.43pm

SUNDAY
21st JULY

morning

afternoon

FULL MOON IN
Capricorn
Toronto - 6.16am, London - 11.16am,
Sydney - 8.16pm

SUN IN CANCER THEN LEO OPPOSITE PLUTO IN AQUARIUS
Today through 25th July

SUN IN CANCER TRINE NEPTUNE IN PISCES
Today through 23rd July

MARS ENTERS GEMINI
Sydney - 6.43am

Radiantly Individuating

THE FIFTH HOUSE - FIXED FIRE
PLANETARY RULER - SUN

Toronto, London & Sydney 22nd July - 23rd August

The dewy emotions of the Moon's domain evaporate as the morning Sun rises where He shines the brightest. He is at home in the constellation of the Lion.

Shining for all living beings, He is the central star around which we revolve and evolve. In astrology, Leo rules the heart, the core of our being, and it's time to breath out the shadows of doubt, fear and anxiety.

Have you forgotten how truly unique you are? There's nobody like you. The Leo Sun invites you to turn towards Him, to tune into your own individual-radiating frequency and align with your authentic self. As you realign, you become like a lit beacon, beaming encouragement to those around you to peel away from the noise of the pack and to become more fully themselves.

There is a healthy competitive urge under the influence of Leo, but not in this aspect. As each individual is illumined by their guiding genius, new harmonics are intoned. Single notes become chords, melodies emerge and roll into symphonies, each note integral to the whole.

Solar energy isn't chaotic; it's serene in the way that the big principles are.
Love, honour, dignity, integrity, conviction and courage, to name a few favoured by Leo.
There's an order to things, a natural progression.
If we get lost in our feelings or burdened by a quagmire of preconditions (be it from society or our own social groups), we find solace in the certainty inherent in our ideals.

Just as we feel the warmth of the Sun when we turn to meet Him, so too can we turn our hearts back to our guiding principles... and meet them again and again, even if we falter and lose our way. The Sun shines for one and all, showing us how to grow in love beyond the trap of small heartedness.

Leo season

CONSIDERATIONS

What are my guiding ideals?
When do I feel the happiest?
When am I my most authentic self?
Do I allow myself and others to individuate?

MERCURY

IN *Virgo*

Enters 26th July
Turns retrograde - 5th August
Leaves Virgo -14th August
Re Enters Virgo - 9th September
Leaves Virgo - 26th September

For this visit, Mercury has an unusual journey through Virgo. He'll turn retrograde and revisit some unfinished business in Leo, before wrapping things up and returning to his home town in Virgo.

THE MESSENGER

Mercury influences how we transmit and receive information, our ideas and conversations as well as influencing movement, trade and travel.

Mercury has two homes. One in Gemini, which we experienced earlier in the year, and the other in earthy Virgo. In Gemini, he relished quick wits, snazzy conversations and a world of ideas. When in Virgo, his analytical, systematic, logistical and organisational sides step into action.

This is not so much about enjoying a satisfying meal (hello Taurus) as it is about precisely following instructions: What system to use to store recipes? Are the herbs easily accessible? And do the matching canisters keep them preserved? It's not that Virgo doesn't like quality. Not at all, he is just as pedantic on that front as well – it's just that how can you enjoy life, or any of its component pieces, when chaos reigns?

This obsession with process and order isn't for everyone, but, we all have to come to terms with the chores. Mercury in Virgo will school you in efficient management in any category.

If a loved one goes full OCD during this time, maybe watch with curiosity and an open mind, and be amazed at their very particular skill set. It's possible that EVERYTHING may get a makeover.

A brilliant time for tackling study, organising cupboards, accounting, recycling clutter, teaching and presentations.

Brilliant manager – Micro manager
Systematic and logical – Nit picky
Quality control – Judgemental

I'VE BEEN THINKING ABOUT...
I JUST WANT TO SAY...

3rd QUARTER MOON

Taurus

REFLECT & RELEASE

27th July - Toronto 10.51pm
28th July - London 3.51am, Sydney 12.51pm

What have you been working towards? The Taurus Moon speaks of a conundrum. On the one hand if you keep working and get a little more saved, you know you'll be better off in the long run. On the other hand, that's a lot of pushing and hustling. What's to stop you enjoying the fruits of your labour right here, right now?

WHAT ARE YOU ASKED TO PUSH THROUGH AND WHAT DO YOU NEED TO RELEASE AS WE HEAD INTO NEXT WEEK'S NEW MOON?

The week ahead

M

T

W

T

F

S

S

morning

afternoon

The weekly transits

Sun enters Leo
Third Quarter Moon in Taurus
Mercury enters Virgo

SUN ENTERS LEO
Toronto - 3.45am, London - 8.45am,
Sydney - 5.45pm

TUESDAY
23rd JULY

morning

afternoon

WEDNESDAY
24th JULY

morning

afternoon

MOON ENTERS
PISCES
Toronto - 9.23am, London - 2.23pm,
Sydney - 11.23pm

THURSDAY
25th JULY

morning

afternoon

FRIDAY
26th JULY

morning

afternoon

MOON ENTERS ARIES
Toronto - 10.52am,
London - 3.52pm, Sydney - 12.52am

MERCURY ENTERS VIRGO
Toronto - 6.42pm, London - 11.42pm

MERCURY ENTERS VIRGO
Sydney - 8.42am

SATURDAY
27th JULY

morning

_____
_____
_____
_____
_____
_____

afternoon

_____
_____
_____
_____
_____
_____
_____
_____

SUNDAY
28th JULY

morning

_____
_____
_____
_____
_____
_____

afternoon

_____
_____
_____
_____
_____
_____
_____
_____

3rd QUARTER MOON
IN *Taurus*
Toronto - 10.51pm

3rd QUARTER MOON
IN *Taurus*
London - 3.51am, Sydney - 12.51pm

NEW MOON

Leo

PLANTING SEEDS

4th August - Toronto 7.11am,
London 12.11am, Sydney 9.11pm

Sun and Moon meet in the privacy of the dark night and it's time to re-set.
Hand on heart, honest to the good truth, how are you?

Gently now, plant your seeds. This one here, a little spark – may it grow into
a roaring enthusiasm and fill you with the courage to live life fully. And this
one, a sweet, little glowing seed, may it blossom in your heart with a love
so expansive that it touches all you meet. And the next one, quiet and pale
like an ember, may it light your way, kindling the inner certainty that comes
from following your highest ideals.

*New Moon in Leo themes: Honour, integrity, nobility, love, play, coming
home to our hearts.*

NEW MOON INTENTIONS

Transits

VENUS IN LEO TRINE CHIRON IN ARIES

28th July through 4th of August
Heightened Influence 30th July through 1st August

We know that women have made progress in society.
But is this the case for the feminine? The Venus in us receives and
magnetises. When we chase and hustle, we're utillising Mars energy.
Venus and Chiron have opened a line of communication.
How do we give space to honour the feminine in ourselves and in each
other? Invite in the healing vibes – be ready to receive. Let it flow.

SUN IN LEO TRINE NORTH NODE IN ARIES
AND SEXTILE SOUTH NODE IN GEMINI

27th July through 4th of August
Heightened Influence 30th July through 1st August

Opportunity streams to us from the future, and a burst of energy highlights
the path ahead. Keep the naysaying-inner-whispers at bay; listen for the
voice that reminds you that you're ready and prepared. Mental work done in
the past is looking to mature and progress.

VENUS IN LEO SQUARE URANUS IN TAURUS

30th July through 6th August
Heightened Influence 2nd through 4th August

Venus is determined and she knows her mind. She's walking her own path
confidently visible in the evening sky, but that doesn't mean she is without
challenges. They won't hold her up though – she's learnt the wisdom of
patience and timing. She'll hold the course no matter the curious obstacles
that vie for her attention.

The week ahead

M

T

W

T

F

S

S

The weekly transits

Venus in Leo trine Chiron in Aries
Sun in Leo trine North Node in
Aries and sextile
South Node in Gemini
Venus in Leo trine Chiron in Aries
New Moon in Leo

morning

afternoon

M O O N   E N T E R S   G E M I N I
Toronto - 5.28pm, London - 10.28pm

TUESDAY
30th JULY

morning

afternoon

MOON ENTERS GEMINI
Sydney - 7.28am

VENUS IN LEO TRINE CHIRON IN ARIES
Today through 1st August

SUN IN LEO TRINE NORTH NODE IN ARIES AND SEXTILE SOUTH NODE IN GEMINI
Today through 1st August

WEDNESDAY
31st JULY

morning

afternoon

MOON ENTERS CANCER
Toronto - 11.19pm

THURSDAY
1st AUGUST

morning

afternoon

FRIDAY
2nd AUGUST

morning

afternoon

**MOON ENTERS
CANCER**

London - 4.19pm, Sydney - 1.19pm

**VENUS IN LEO
SQUARE CHIRON IN
ARIES**

Today through 4th August

SATURDAY
3rd AUGUST

morning

afternoon

MOON ENTERS LEO
Toronto - 7.10am, London - 12.10pm,
Sydney - 9.10pm

SUNDAY
4th AUGUST

morning

afternoon

NEW MOON IN *Leo*
Toronto - 7.11am, London - 12.11pm,
Sydney - 9.11pm

**VENUS ENTERS
VIRGO**

VENUS
in *Virgo*

Toronto, London & Sydney 5th August - 29th August

THE MUSE
Venus works in the sphere of love, desire, creativity and relationships.
She influences our personal magnetism, tastes and resources.

LOVE AND DESIRE
Venus steps through the door and checks that things are in order. Her heart
longs for an elegant simplicity and a purity of feeling.

CREATIVITY AND INSPIRATION
The chaotic mass of modern life with its random noises and mess can be a
lot – especially for one as sensitive as Venus. She finds inspiration in classic,
functional-yet-beautiful spaces and in pristine ecosystems. She is a chemist,
a botanist and a nurse; her lotions and potions work miracles.

THE MANNER OF RELATING
Her taste is beyond reproach. If you are encountering her essence, either
through a person or if you, yourself, can feel her instructive influence in
your life – well done! She's considered and choosy. You've made the grade.
Welcome to a beautiful, refined and intelligent world.

Purity as an aesthetic - Aloof
Health conscious - Obsessively so
Tasteful - Judgemental

I'M SO INSPIRED BY… I LOVE…
IT DRIVES ME CRAZY WHEN…
EXPLORE WHEN THE MOOD STRIKES

MERCURY RETROGRADE
BEGINNING IN VIRGO THEN
WITH THE MAJORITY IN
Leo

Toronto:
Mercury Retrograde in Virgo - 5th August, Mercury Re - enters Leo - 14th August, Mercury stations - 26th August, Mercury turns direct - 28th August, Mercury Re - enters Virgo - 9th September, Free! Leaves the Shadow Zone - 12th September

London:
Mercury Retrograde in Virgo - 5th August, Mercury Re - enters Leo - 15th August, Mercury stations - 26th August, Mercury turns direct - 28th August, Mercury Re - enters Virgo - 9th September, Free! Leaves the Shadow Zone - 12th September

Sydney:
Mercury Retrograde in Virgo - 5th August, Mercury Re - enters Leo - 15th August, Mercury stations - 26th August, Mercury turns direct - 29th August, Mercury Re - enters Virgo - 9th September, Free! Leaves the Shadow Zone - 12th September

It's that special time again. Mercury has been organising everyone's life as he travels through Virgo, only to realise that something very close to the heart has been forgotten. What do you need to retrieve as he forays into Leo?

Mercury retro rules apply – it's best to avoid signing important contracts, releasing projects and anything else where easy, clean momentum is desired. If you're already scheduled, go with it, and treat any hiccups as the humorous side to Mercury retro... If you can!

INSIGHTS OVER THE COURSE OF THIS
MERCURY RETROGRADE IN VIRGO,
THEN IN LEO AND VIRGO AGAIN

The week ahead

M

T

W

T

F

S

S

MONDAY
5th AUGUST

morning

afternoon

The weekly transits

Venus enters Virgo
Mercury goes Retrograde in Virgo
Mars conjunct Jupiter in Gemini

VENUS ENTERS VIRGO
London - 3.23pm, Sydney - 12.23pm

MERCURY GOES RETROGRADE IN VIRGO
Toronto - 12.56am, London - 5.56am,
Sydney - 2.56pm

TUESDAY
6th AUGUST

morning

afternoon

WEDNESDAY
7th AUGUST

morning

afternoon

MOON ENTERS
VIRGO
Toronto - 5.17pm, London - 10.17pm,
Sydney - 7.17am

THURSDAY
8th AUGUST

morning

afternoon

FRIDAY
9th AUGUST

morning

afternoon

MOON ENTERS LIBRA
Toronto - 5.31am, London - 10.31am,
Sydney - 7.31pm

SATURDAY
10th AUGUST

morning

afternoon

SUNDAY
11th AUGUST

morning

afternoon

MOON ENTERS SCORPIO
Toronto - 6.34am, London - 11.34pm,
Sydney - 8.34pm

1st QUARTER MOON

Scorpio

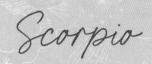

MOMENTUM & GROWTH

12th August - Toronto 10.19am, London 3.19pm
13th August - Sydney 1.19am

There is nowhere to hide from the Scorpio Moon. She can see everything. Does that mean she's going to blab your confidential information all over town? Absolutely not! If anyone knows the value of secrets, it's Scorpio. There may be a price to pay, but not for her silence. Even though she sees and comprehends all, don't confuse her as the sum total of everybody's secrets – she hungers to be recognised in her right.

WHAT ACTIONS AM I TAKING TO FULFIL INTENTIONS SET ON THE NEW MOON?

Transits

SUN CONJUNCT
MERCURY RETROGRADE IN LEO

16th through 22nd of August
Heightened Influence 18th through 20th August

An encounter from the past arrives bringing updated information. Hold off from forming a rash judgement – you still don't have all the info.

VENUS IN VIRGO
OPPOSITE SATURN IN PISCES

16th through 24th August
Heightened Influence 18th through 21st August

There is a tendency, with Virgo energy, to delve into the minutiae. Our focus can get smaller and tighter as we become fixated on component parts. Saturn over in Pisces (the wise man of the sea) is reminding us of the big picture. All masterpieces are created from the marriage of skill and imagination... and time.

The week ahead

M

T

W

T

F

S

S

The weekly transits

First Quarter Moon in Scorpio
Mercury Retrograde re enters Leo
Sun conjunct Mercury Retrograde in Leo
Venus in Virgo opposite Saturn in Pisces

morning

afternoon

1st QUARTER MOON
IN *Scorpio*
Toronto - 10.19am, London - 3.19pm

TUESDAY
13th AUGUST

morning

afternoon

WEDNESDAY
14th AUGUST

morning

afternoon

1st QUARTER MOON
IN *Scorpio*
Sydney - 1.19am

MOON ENTERS SAGITTARIUS
Toronto - 6.01am, London - 11.01am,
Sydney - 8.01pm

THURSDAY
15th AUGUST

morning

afternoon

MERCURY RETROGRADE RE ENTERS LEO

FRIDAY
16th AUGUST

morning

afternoon

MOON ENTERS CAPRICORN
Toronto - 1.51pm, London - 6.51pm, Sydney - 3.51am

morning

afternoon

MOON ENTERS
AQUARIUS
Toronto - 5.45pm, London - 10.45pm

morning

afternoon

MOON ENTERS
AQUARIUS
Sydney - 7.45am

SUN CONJUNCT
MERCURY
RETROGRADE IN LEO
Today through 20th

VENUS IN VIRGO
OPPOSITE SATURN
IN PISCES
Today through 21st August

PEAK ENERGY,
BLESSINGS & BLOSSOMS

19th August Toronto 7.26pm, London 7.26pm,
20th August Sydney 4.26am

Some Full Moons have a dose more lunacy then others and this one
has curious energy to it. The Aquarian Moon shouts out to the Leo Sun,
reminding him that individuals have to work TOGETHER. It's not that He's
forgotten, it's just that Mercury is revisiting and has something to tell Him.
Uranus, impatiently working his way through the final degrees of Taurus, is
pushing his point. Change of direction? Realignment? A choice to be made?
There sure is a din. How's it playing out for you?

HOW HAVE INTENTIONS
MADE ON THE NEW MOON MANIFESTED?

_____

_____

_____

_____

_____

_____

The week ahead

M

T

W

T

F

S

S

The weekly transits

Full Moon in Aquarius

MONDAY
19th AUGUST

MONDAY
19th AUGUST

morning

afternoon

FULL MOON IN
Aquarius
Toronto - 2.26pm, London - 7.26pm

morning

afternoon

morning

afternoon

FULL MOON IN
Aquarius
Sydney - 4.26am

MOON ENTERS PISCES
Toronto - 6.52pm, London - 11.52pm

MOON ENTERS PISCES
Sydney - 8.52am

MOON ENTERS ARIES
Toronto - 7.02pm

THURSDAY
22nd AUGUST

morning

afternoon

MOON ENTERS ARIES
London - 12.02am, Sydney - 9.02am

FRIDAY
23rd AUGUST

morning

afternoon

SUN ENTERS VIRGO
Toronto - 10.55am, London - 3.55pm,
Sydney - 12.55am

MOON ENTERS TAURUS
Toronto - 8.00pm

afternoon

afternoon

MOON ENTERS
TAURUS
London - 1.00am, Sydney - 10.00am

SUN IN VIRGO

Service, Loving Discernment & Intelligent Process

THE SIXTH HOUSE - MUTABLE EARTH
PLANETARY RULER - MERCURY

Toronto, London & Sydney 23rd August - 22nd September

The expansive brushstrokes of the Leo Sun pass into the exactitudes of Virgo. We know she has high standards, but why?

The Virgin stands in her field of stars, like a traditional healer in a meadow of wildflowers. She picks, sifts and sorts them into categories, humming as she bundles them. She gathers wax and honey from the bees and roots out buried tubers with the reverence of a priestess. She pauses as she thinks through the next phase – the transformation of nature's outpouring into medicine.

Virgo stands opposite the constellation of the Fish, and where Pisces swim in the oneness of creation, she counterbalances with understanding that everything comes in and out of being through a series of processes. There is a natural order to all things.

She studies this. Observing with a scientific exactitude – If there's a right way to do things, that means there's also the possibility of error. This thorny fact bothers her and spurs her ever onwards in her quest for perfection.

How can we serve others, and heal the splintering rifts that repeatedly manifest, if we don't believe that we can find a cure?

Virgo teaches us to delve deeply into the processes that make up our lives. She sees each one as a type of story – with a beginning, middle and an accomplishment at the end. How could we ever be bored when there are so many stories unfolding that we can influence? How can we settle into dis-ease when there is always an antidote to be found and applied?

Virgo season
CONSIDERATIONS

What set of processes do I favour?
Which ones do I shy away from?
Where do I serve others and where am I served?
Am I taking care of myself?

VENUS

IN *Libra*

Toronto 29th August - 22nd September
London, Sydney 29th August - 23rd September

THE MUSE
Venus works in the sphere of love, desire, creativity and relationships. She influences our personal magnetism, tastes and resources.

LOVE AND DESIRE
Venus comes home to her realm. She is serenely confident and at ease. Seeking beauty, harmony and open communication in her personal as well as professional life. These are non-negotiable.

CREATIVITY AND INSPIRATION
To connect with Venus in Libra, look to beauty and balance. This is a time for creative and artistic ventures.
Fashion, interior design, graphics, flowers... Anything that transforms our environment, and us, into a thing of beauty and elegance.

THE MANNER OF RELATING
The Libran Venus is both a light, airy social butterfly and a thoughtful and considered being. She is skilled in the art of communication; verbally adept but also a master of subtle body language. She definitely knows the secret code and meaning of flowers and what gift to give on the various years of anniversaries.

Bright and social – Snobbish and discriminatory
Thoughtful – Emotionally aloof
Creative – Unfinished projects may mount up

I'M SO INSPIRED BY... I LOVE...
IT DRIVES ME CRAZY WHEN...
EXPLORE WHEN THE MOOD STRIKES

3rd QUARTER MOON

Gemini

REFLECT & RELEASE

26th August - Toronto 5.26am,
London 10.26am, Sydney 7.26pm

Oh chatty Gemini Moon you have a lot to say tonight! Mars and Jupiter have been spurring each other on with alarming force, and it's time to feel the impact. Take the opportunity, if it should present, to have the conversations needed; you'll find the words.

As the Moon winds down, wouldn't it be great to be able to wind down with her? Leave the stress behind. For a minute. You won't miss out.

WHAT HAVE I ACHIEVED
AND WHAT DO I NEED TO RELEASE?

Transits

VENUS IN VIRGO (THEN INTO LIBRA) OPPOSITE NEPTUNE IN PISCES

25th August through 2nd September
Heightened Influence 28th through 31st August

Venus garnered Saturn's sound advice and decides that, before committing to anything serious, she needs a holiday. Neptune is happy to oblige. Hearts expand, love is felt, guards are let down and sweet words are spoken.

VENUS IN VIRGO (THEN INTO LIBRA) TRINE PLUTO IN AQUARIUS

26th August through 2nd of September
Heightened Influence 28th through 31st August

Magnetised by open channels of communication with Pluto, Venus is hard to resist. What's more compelling than a beautiful, empowered woman? Watch for a message from the past early to mid week.

The week ahead

M

T

W

T

F

S

S

The weekly transits

Third Quarter Moon in Gemini
Mercury stations in Leo
Venus in Virgo (then into Libra)
opposite Neptune in Pisces
Venus in Virgo (then into Libra)
trine Pluto in Aquarius
Mercury goes Direct
Venus enters Leo

MONDAY
26th AUGUST

morning

afternoon

3rd QUARTER MOON
IN *Gemini*

Toronto - 5.26am, London - 10.26am,
Sydney - 7.26pm

MERCURY STATIONS IN LEO

Toronto - 2.50am, London - 7.50am,
Sydney - 4.58pm

TUESDAY
27th AUGUST

morning

afternoon

WEDNESDAY
28th AUGUST

morning

afternoon

MOON ENTERS CANCER
Toronto - 4.47am, London - 9.47am,
Sydney - 6.47pm

VENUS IN VIRGO (AND THEN INTO LIBRA) OPPOSITE NEPTUNE IN PISCES
Today through 31st August

THURSDAY
29th AUGUST

morning

afternoon

MERCURY GOES DIRECT

VENUS ENTERS LIBRA
Toronto - 9.23am, London - 2.23pm,
Sydney - 11.23pm

FRIDAY
30th AUGUST

morning

afternoon

MOON ENTERS LEO
Toronto - 1.09pm, London - 6.09pm

SATURDAY
31st AUGUST

morning

....

....

....

....

....

afternoon

....

....

....

....

....

MOON ENTERS LEO

Sydney - 3.09am

SUNDAY
1st SEPTEMBER

morning

....

....

....

....

....

afternoon

....

....

....

....

....

MOON ENTERS VIRGO

Toronto - 1.48pm

MARS

IN *Cancer*

Toronto, London 4th September - 4th November
Sydney 3rd September - 4th November

THE WARRIOR

Mars works through our drives and desires; our ambitions and how we achieve them. He sets and secures our personal boundaries and defends us against those who transgress them.

DRIVES AND DESIRES

Mars derives satisfaction when he is of assistance to others. Once he adjusts to all the feels of the Cancerian realm, you'll find him caring for the disenfranchised, abandoned and forgotten souls.

AMBITION AND WORK

Mars wants to make a difference in people's lives and he does, but he's also practical and finds a way to support himself in the process. He has a way of resurrecting the past's forgotten dreams and projects – be it through renovation and restoration, or reviving forgotten aesthetics.

BOUNDARIES AND PROTECTION

He tries anger, and then passive aggression, until he learns to express the deeper aspects of himself that usually stay locked away... as if asking him to reveal his heart is an act of aggression. Fair enough. Emotional boundaries can be the hardest to set. It takes practice.

When Mars is in Cancer you may experience: Emotional resilience and heightened intuition, passion and protective impulses.

Difficulties you may encounter: Tendencies toward defensive, evasive or passive-aggressive behaviours.

INTENTIONS, INSIGHTS & ACCOMPLISHMENTS

NEW MOON

Virgo

PLANTING SEEDS

3rd September - Toronto 9.55pm,
London 2.55am, Sydney 11.55am

The bond between Grandchild and Grandparent is a special one.
Fresh from the world of spirit the child brings open-hearted innocence and
love. Rich with life experience, the Grandparent has been released from the
egoistic battle of youth – hopefully.

They don't meet in the middle, more on an entirely different plane. When
the Grandparent hands the bairn back to the parent they watch their own,
now adult child, get put through the gauntlet that they, during their turn,
put you through.

Meanwhile it's all mud pies, songs, tales and tea parties. Also gardening, toy
cars and tinkering... What innocent joy!
The energy of this New Moon speaks to the affinity between the old and the
young – and pure love found in unusual places.

NEW MOON INTENTIONS

....

....

....

....

Transits

SUN IN VIRGO OPPOSITE SATURN IN PISCES

4th through 13th of September
Heightened Influence 7th through 10th September

Even research shows that 'acts of kindness are linked to increased feelings of wellbeing'. Likewise, receiving help – no matter how independent we may have become, facilitates the growth of trust, in turn deepening and strengthening bonds of friendship. Maintaining an attitude of gratitude, whether you are the helper or the helpee will keep the love flowing, even if challenges are being faced.

SUN IN VIRGO SQUARE JUPITER IN GEMINI

7th through 17th of September
Heightened Influence 11th through 14th September

Funny thing about opportunities is that they can pass you by.
Might be you were distracted on a phone call.
Maybe you assumed it would still be there if the current thing fell through.
Possibly you got all inflated and felt yourself just a little too strongly.

Take a look at what's been presented... It promises to be life-expanding and joyous. Collect your wits, tune in, two feet on the earth and say 'YES'; if it's what you really want – go for it.

The week ahead

M

_____

T

_____

W

_____

T

_____

F

_____

S

_____

S

_____

The weekly transits

Pluto retrograde re-enters Capricorn
New Moon in Virgo
Mars enters Cancer
Sun in Virgo opposite Saturn in Pisces

MONDAY
2nd SEPTEMBER

morning

_____

_____

_____

afternoon

_____

_____

_____

NEW MOON IN *Virgo*
Toronto - 9.55pm

MOON ENTERS VIRGO
London - 4.48am, Sydney - 1.48pm

PLUTO RETROGRADE RE-ENTERS CAPRICORN

TUESDAY
3rd SEPTEMBER

morning

afternoon

NEW MOON IN *Virgo*
Toronto - 9.55pm, London - 2.55am,
Sydney - 11.55am

WEDNESDAY
4th SEPTEMBER

morning

afternoon

MARS ENTERS
CANCER
Toronto - 3.46pm, London - 8.46pm

MOON ENTERS LIBRA
Toronto - 12.12pm, London - 5.12pm

THURSDAY
5th SEPTEMBER

morning

afternoon

FRIDAY
6th SEPTEMBER

morning

afternoon

MOON ENTERS LIBRA
Sydney - 2.12am

MARS ENTERS CANCER
Sydney - 5.46am

SATURDAY
7th SEPTEMBER

morning

afternoon

SUNDAY
8th SEPTEMBER

morning

afternoon

MOON ENTERS SCORPIO
Toronto - 1.18am, London - 6.18am,
Sydney - 3.18pm

SUN IN VIRGO OPPOSITE SATURN IN PISCES
Today through 10th September

1st QUARTER MOON

Sagittarius

MOMENTUM & GROWTH

11th September - Toronto 2.05am,
London 7.05am, Sydney 4.05pm

Wow. The tension is freaking palpable. Someone is itching to break free. Like, get me out of here, you're killing me with boredom. Do you really want to hammer me down until all that's left is a soulless robot stuck on a repeating schedule of chores!?

Take the break. It doesn't mean your whole life has to be chucked out. Could be a weekend will do it – or a little imagination. The ingredients that make up your life could bake an entirely different cake. Then again, you might end up on an entirely new continent.

WHAT ACTIONS AM I TAKING TO FULFIL INTENTIONS SET ON THE NEW MOON?

MERCURY

RE-ENTERS *Virgo*

Toronto, London & Sydney 9th September - 26th September

It's been a long journey since Mercury first entered Virgo, back on the 26th July. What a detour! But, he's back home now - but only for a few weeks. He flies through Virgo at light speed. Instead of going into detail (flick back through to late July to find the full description) here are the main Mercury in Virgo themes.

Excellence in logic and practical comprehension. Think engineers and textbook writers – being factually based, favouring workable targets and attainable goals. If you have any sizable task to accomplish now, is the time to break it down into component parts and make lists within lists. It does need to be achieved in the next few weeks, but this is such a great time to prioritise and organise long-term objectives.

HOW AM I GOING TO MAKE THE MOST OF MERCURY'S TRANSIT THROUGH VIRGO?

The week ahead

M

T

W

T

F

S

S

The weekly transits

First Quarter Moon in Sagittarius
Sun in Virgo square Jupiter in Gemini
Mercury re-enters Virgo

MONDAY
9th SEPTEMBER

morning

afternoon

MERCURY
RE-ENTERS VIRGO

MOON ENTERS
SAGITTARIUS
Toronto - 1.26pm, London - 6.26pm

TUESDAY
10th SEPTEMBER

morning

afternoon

**MOON ENTERS
SAGITTARIUS**

Sydney - 3.26am

WEDNESDAY
11th SEPTEMBER

morning

afternoon

1st QUARTER MOON

IN *Sagittarius*

Toronto - 2.05am, London - 7.05am,
Sydney - 4.05pm

**SUN IN VIRGO
SQUARE
JUPITER IN GEMINI**

Today through 14th September

**MOON ENTERS
CAPRICORN**

Toronto - 10.38pm

morning

afternoon

**MOON ENTERS
CAPRICORN**
London - 3.38am, Sydney - 12.38pm

**MERCURY LEAVES
THE SHADOW ZONE**

morning

afternoon

SATURDAY
14th SEPTEMBER

morning

afternoon

SUNDAY
15th SEPTEMBER

morning

afternoon

MOON ENTERS
AQUARIUS
Toronto - 5.36am, London - 10.36am,
Sydney - 7.36pm

FULL MOON

Pisces

PEAK ENERGY,
BLESSINGS & BLOSSOMS

17th September - Toronto 10.33pm
18th September - London 3.33am, Sydney

The balance and harmony in the cosmic rhythm never disappoints.
We've been travelling with the Sun in Virgo for three weeks now.
The exacting standards can fray the nerves of those not naturally inclined
to be endlessly practical. Just when we think we can't fold another
tea towel, the pendulum swings, taking us with it. Contrary to Virgo's belief
that everything can be thought through and controlled, the Pisces'
Eclipse Moon shouts out in full lunatic mode.

*"It'll work out ok and, if not, who really cares, in this instance?
It's you, me, and right now, right here."*

We're all on an expansive bender, and by the end of it we'll have reconnected
individually and collectively, to the mythic journey we're on. Ride the wave, but
be aware that any addictive tendencies may be amplified.

HOW WAS YOUR NIGHT?

MUSINGS

Transits

VENUS IN LIBRA OPPOSITE CHIRON IN ARIES

14th through 21st September
Heightened Influence 16th through 18th September

How sweet is harmony? It's almost invisible, yet once it's achieved and, in some cases earnt, shouldn't we be entitled for it to last? Chiron in Aries doesn't want to be rude about it, but something needs to be addressed. Are all the individuals concerned happy? Has someone sacrificed themselves for the good of the whole? Have you? Just a little rebalancing needed.

SUN IN VIRGO OPPOSITE NEPTUNE IN PISCES

17th through 25th September
Heightened Influence 19th through 23rd September

Have you noticed a theme with the transits? First Saturn and then Neptune a week or so later. These two create a curious mix. Saturn wants to consolidate and form. Neptune wants to dematerialise and mystify. Up and down. Sad and then happy. This year we are acclimatising to this swinging-energy pattern, next year they'll set the mood as they finally conjunct. For this current transit, you may notice that the smaller details that you've been focused on give way to a much larger, dreamier vision. It's a hard rip to swim against it; where is the tide pulling you?

Grand Earth Trine

SUN IN VIRGO
TRINE PLUTO IN CAPRICORN
TRINE URANUS IN TAURUS

16th through 26th of September

Heightened Influence 19th through 24th September

A grand trine is an aspect where three planets (or more) are at the same degree in the same element. It is considered a beneficial transit where energy flows freely. It's been said about trines that you can miss them as they aren't in your face; they're the part of life that's going well and therefore there can be a tendency to take them for granted. You don't have to work hard for it and it's not one of those 'the benefit is in the growth' situations. Let's separate out the strands.

THE SUN IN VIRGO – Our capacity to untangle complex situations, to serve ourselves and others through the use of intelligent, logical and practical processes.

URANUS IN TAURUS – Mother Earth's magic. Connecting and learning from natural elements in surprising ways. Also, finding freedom from long, drawn-out life patterns.

PLUTO IN CAPRICORN (FINAL VISIT) – Taking your personal power back from overwhelming control mechanisms and systems that don't have your best interest at heart (or anywhere else).

HOW'S THIS FLOWING FOR YOU?
CAN YOU SEPARATE OUT THESE STRANDS
IN YOUR LIFE AND FIND THE THEME?

The week ahead

M

T

W

T

F

S

S

morning

afternoon

The weekly transits

Venus in Libra opposite Chiron in Aries
Full Moon in Pisces
Sun in Virgo opposite Neptune in Pisces
Grand Earth Trine – Sun in Virgo trine
Pluto in Capricorn trine Uranus in Taurus

MOON ENTERS PISCES
Toronto - 5.39am, London - 10.39am,
Sydney - 7.39pm

TUESDAY
17th SEPTEMBER

morning

afternoon

FULL MOON IN
Pisces
Toronto - 10.33pm

WEDNESDAY
18th SEPTEMBER

morning

afternoon

FULL MOON IN *Pisces*
London - 3.33am, Sydney - 12.33pm

MOON ENTERS ARIES
Toronto - 5.24am, London - 10.24am,
Sydney - 7.24pm

morning

morning

afternoon

afternoon

**SUN IN VIRGO
OPPOSITE
NEPTUNE IN PISCES**
Today through 23rd September

**GRAND EARTH TRINE
– SUN IN VIRGO
TRINE PLUTO IN
CAPRICORN TRINE
URANUS IN TAURUS**
Today through 24th September

**MOON ENTERS
TAURUS**
Toronto - 5.03am, London - 10.03am,
Sydney - 7.03pm

SATURDAY
21st SEPTEMBER

morning

afternoon

SUNDAY
22nd SEPTEMBER

morning

afternoon

SUN ENTERS LIBRA
Toronto - 8.44am, London - 1.44pm,
Sydney - 10.44pm

MOON ENTERS GEMINI
Toronto - 6.24am, London - 11.24am,
Sydney - 8.24pm

**VENUS ENTERS
SCORPIO**
Toronto - 10.36pm

SUN IN LIBRA
The Fine Art of Balance

THE SEVENTH HOUSE - CARDINAL AIR
PLANETARY RULER - VENUS

Toronto, London & Sydney 22nd September - 22nd October

Libra is depicted as the scales and there are always two sides where Libra is concerned. She shows us a way through the complex fragmentation of duality.

Self and other, good and bad, beautiful and ugly, black and white. She weighs and measures all information and seeks a just fairness and balance at all times. This sounds severe, but she has a light touch. Venus rules this domain – think gentle conversations and time deliberating on the multiple viewpoints of any given situation. It can take a while, there's a lot of talking. She earnestly wants to get it right and have all parties happy.

In ancient Egypt it was perceived that the Gods performed a rite after death in order to know which path a soul should be sent along. The Heart retained all the good and harmful deeds carried out over the course of a life. If the good deeds outweighed the bad; the Heart would balance with the Feather of Order, Truth and Justice and then the soul would be free to journey onto the next life.

Nowadays, our conscience is the feather of truth. We're given the opportunity to rebalance our Hearts at the end of every day. We can explore our souls and ask ourselves a series of questions. Is my conscience niggling or am I satisfied with my actions today? Is there any unfinished business? Did someone misunderstand an intention. Did my actions cause harm? If so, how can I amend this?

Where social conscience is lacking Libra gives voice to the silenced.
She seeks balance and harmony, not retribution.
She doesn't seek revenge, rather resolution.

Libra season
CONSIDERATIONS

How is my relationship with my conscience?
Am I too hard on myself or do I let myself off too easily?
What's my conflict resolution style?
I would like to harness the Libran energy to...

....

....

....

....

....

....

....

....

....

....

....

....

....

VENUS

IN *Scorpio*

Toronto, London & Sydney 22nd September - 18th October

THE MUSE

Venus works in the sphere of love, desire, creativity and relationships. She influences our personal magnetism, tastes and resources.

LOVE AND DESIRE

Her love is powerful and fully embodied. She'll commit to projects and relationships once she's certain that they can hold her intensity – and give her the room she needs to explore the psychic realms. She's dedicated to her loves, whichever form they come in.

CREATIVITY AND INSPIRATION

Venus is magnetically hypnotising ... Inspiring and adoring music that lulls and entices, songs that mesmerise and conjure feelings from the depths. Her interests may include the Tarot, the uncovering of hidden or forgotten truths and ritual. She is highly intuitive and empathic.

THE MANNER OF RELATING

Clearly, the shallows don't interest her, she needs to delve deep, ever deeper. What are you really feeling, what secrets do you harbour? What obstacles have you overcome and how have you transformed?

Deeply caring – But not if she doesn't like you!
Magnetic – Manipulative
Loyal – Possessive

I'M SO INSPIRED BY... I LOVE...
IT DRIVES ME CRAZY WHEN...
EXPLORE WHEN THE MOOD STRIKES

MERCURY

IN *Libra*

Toronto, London 26 September - 13 October
Sydney 26 September - 14 October

THE MESSENGER

Mercury influences how we transmit and receive information, our ideas and conversations as well as influencing movement, trade and travel.

Mercury in Libra is the ultimate diplomat. He can size up a situation, capturing the subtle moods of those concerned faster than you can say 'get lost – I don't care'. He has a lot to say on the matter, and we'd be wise to listen, if we want a fair outcome. He seeks balance and harmony in all of his relationships and works hard to attain it. His listening ear is always ready – and it's not just for show. He is invested. He has hours up his sleeve and he's willing to spend them hearing every last detail – from multiple perspectives. How else is he going to come up with that brilliant win-win outcome?

He listens well and is solutions-based, often suggesting a little compromise from all parties... It's easy to see the logic here, it sounds fair, but there is a point that an individual can be wobbled, inch by inch away from their position and their integrity. Ultimately his task is to explore all the options – not to decide the outcome.

Mercury in Libra inspires broadminded, inclusive conversations and will help to get any conversation started. He is easy going (when not switched to obsessive-solutions mode) and has a vast social network spread across all demographics of society.

A brilliant time for exploring counselling, balancing the books, reading, expanding the mind and social gatherings.

Diplomat – A people pleaser
Broad minded – Loses his own viewpoint
Socially minded – A gossip

I'VE BEEN THINKING ABOUT...
I JUST WANT TO SAY...

3rd QUARTER MOON

Cancer

REFLECT & RELEASE

24th September - Toronto 2.49pm,
London 7.49pm
25th September - Sydney 4.49am

We are in the final pushing-through phase. Mars is connected to the Moon in Cancer today, so watch for passive-aggressive pressures or emotionally volatile outbursts. Be canny. Do you need to enter the fray?
Also, we are in eclipse season, what has the universe been showing you?

WHAT DO YOU NEED TO RELEASE AS WE HEAD INTO NEXT WEEK'S NEW MOON?

....

....

....

....

....

....

....

....

Transits

MARS IN CANCER
TRINE SATURN IN PISCES

23rd September through 7th of October
Heightened Influence 28th September through 2nd October

When Mars in Cancer and Saturn in Pisces meet, an emotional warrior is born. Taught the old ways by his grandfather, he is deeply compassionate and will battle to protect his kin, and to him, anyone can become clan – the animals, trees, birds and bees. Whomever needs care and safety will find a safe haven in his lands. It may not be playing out in your life in such an arcane way, but what is your inner warrior being called upon to protect?

The week ahead

M

T

W

T

F

S

S

The weekly transits

Sun enters Libra
Venus enters Scorpio
Third Quarter Moon in Cancer
Mercury enters Libra
Mars in Cancer trine Saturn in Pisces

morning

afternoon

**V E N U S   E N T E R S
S C O R P I O**
London - 3.36am, Sydney - 12.36pm

TUESDAY
24th SEPTEMBER

morning

afternoon

3rd QUARTER MOON
IN *Cancer*
Toronto - 2.49pm, London - 7.49pm

WEDNESDAY
25th SEPTEMBER

morning

afternoon

3rd QUARTER MOON
IN *Cancer*
Sydney - 4.49am

THURSDAY
26th SEPTEMBER

morning

afternoon

MERCURY ENTERS LIBRA
Toronto - 4.09am, London - 9.09am,
Sydney - 6.09pm

MOON ENTERS LEO
Toronto - 6.47pm, London - 11.47pm

FRIDAY
27th SEPTEMBER

morning

afternoon

MOON ENTERS LEO
Sydney - 8.47am

SATURDAY
28th SEPTEMBER

morning

afternoon

MARS IN CANCER
TRINE
SATURN IN PISCES
Today through 2nd October

SUNDAY
29th SEPTEMBER

morning

afternoon

MOON ENTERS VIRGO
Toronto - 5.42am, London - 10.42am,
Sydney - 7.42pm

NEW MOON

Libra

SOLAR ECLIPSE
THE ECLIPSE PORTAL CLOSES

2nd October - Toronto 2.48pm, London 7.48pm
3rd October - Sydney 4.48am

In a Solar Eclipse the Moon blocks the light of the Sun and the dark side of the Moon is fully lit. It's like we are out of the conversation, thrown back on our own devices without the radiant guidance of the Sun. When in Libra, themes connected to relationships, friend groups and families come to the fore.

No matter how conscientious we are, all of us have a kind of relationship graveyard loitering in the past. It's filled with the spectres of what wasn't said or done. Those we've hurt or abandoned, or those who ghosted us and caused harm, in any of the billion ways that humans can hurt each other. They lie in wait – waiting for peace and resolution deep in the internal caverns of our soul.

How has it been going since the Eclipse door yawned open? Have you had any unexpected visitors? Have any old stories arisen to fulfil their next chapter? Libra offers us the key to social rebalancing and harmony. Keep the heart open.

THE ECLIPSE PORTAL WHICH HAS BEEN OPEN FOR THE LAST TWO WEEKS GRADUALLY CLOSES. WHAT HAS ENTERED YOUR LIFE? WHO OR WHAT HAS LEFT?

Transits

SUN CONJUNCT SOUTH NODE AND MERCURY IN LIBRA

27th September through 7th October
Heightened Influence 30th September through 3rd October

A messenger pierces through the veil of time. Does the news they bring send you deep into nostalgia, or will it show you the path ahead?

Grand Water Trine

VENUS IN SCORPIO TRINE MARS IN CANCER TRINE SATURN IN PISCES

2nd through 14th October
Heightened Influence 4th through 10th October

When our emotions flow in harmony with our surroundings it's as if we're awash in the gentlest of tides, and warming love and contentment allows us to arrive at deep, profound understanding with ease. Let it flow in. What insights and understandings have awoken in your heart?

SUN IN LIBRA SQUARE MARS IN CANCER SQUARE CHIRON IN ARIES

3rd through 23rd October
Heightened Influence 10th through 17th October

The struggle to maintain much-needed stamina continues. But the more you fight what you're facing, the more energy you expend. Ease into the reality of where you are. This alignment is creating a frustrating, holding pattern – switch your focus to the voice below the frustration. It's talking about change. What else is it saying to you?

The week ahead

M

T

W

T

F

S

S

The weekly transits

Sun conjunct South Node
and Mercury in Libra
New Moon in Libra – Solar Eclipse
Grand Water Trine – Venus
in Scorpio trine Mars in Cancer
trine Saturn in Pisces

morning

afternoon

TUESDAY
1st OCTOBER

morning

....

....

....

....

....

afternoon

....

....

....

....

MOON ENTERS LIBRA
Toronto - 6.20pm, London - 11.20pm

**SUN CONJUNCT
SOUTH NODE AND
MERCURY IN LIBRA**
Today through 3rd October

WEDNESDAY
2nd OCTOBER

morning

....

....

....

....

afternoon

....

....

....

....

MOON ENTERS LIBRA
Sydney - 8.20am

**NEW MOON IN *Libra*
- SOLAR ECLIPSE**
Toronto - 2.48pm, London - 7.48pm

THURSDAY
3rd OCTOBER

morning

....

....

....

....

afternoon

....

....

....

....

....

NEW MOON IN *Libra*
- SOLAR ECLIPSE
Sydney - 4.48am

**SUN IN LIBRA
SQUARE MARS IN
CANCER SQUARE
CHIRON IN ARIES**
Today through 23rd October

FRIDAY
4th OCTOBER

morning

....

....

....

....

afternoon

....

....

....

....

....

**MOON ENTERS
SCORPIO**
Toronto - 6.22am, London - 11.22am,
Sydney - 9.22pm

**VENUS IN SCORPIO
TRINE MARS IN
CANCER TRINE
SATURN IN PISCES**
Today through 10th of October

SATURDAY
5th OCTOBER

morning

....
....
....
....
....

afternoon

....
....
....
....
....
....

SUNDAY
6th OCTOBER

morning

....
....
....
....
....

afternoon

....
....
....
....
....

**MOON ENTERS
SAGITTARIUS**
Toronto - 7.34pm

1st QUARTER MOON

Capricorn

PUSHING THROUGH

10th October - Toronto 1.31pm London 6.31am
11th October - Sydney 4.31pm

There's a real push to the first quarter Moon and this is especially true tonight. The Sun and Moon are squaring Chiron and Mars, forming a fleeting, cardinal grand cross – and Pluto is also involved.

It can feel like a holding pattern where all possible outcomes leave something lacking. But the Moon is in Capricorn, she is resilient and results-focused. Stay the course and find a healthy way to let off any excess tension that you may be feeling.

AM I STILL FEELING THE EFFECTS OF LAST WEEK'S SOLAR ECLIPSE?

WHAT IS PUSHING THROUGH THIS EVENING?

Transits

MARS IN CANCER SQUARE CHIRON IN ARIES

6th October through 22nd of October
Heightened Influence 10th through 16th October

It's easy to see fatigue as an enemy. Exhaustion can be so frustrating, especially when we're under pressure and deadlines and expectations loom large. If you, or a loved one, are struggling to perform at maximum capacity, know that this period will pass and free-flowing energy will return... but no amount of pushing right now will help.

The week ahead

M

T

W

T

F

S

S

The weekly transits

First Quarter Moon in Capricorn
Mars in Cancer square Chiron in Aries
Sun in Libra square Mars in Cancer
square Chiron in Aries

MONDAY
7th OCTOBER

morning

afternoon

MOON ENTERS
SAGITTARIUS
London - 12.34am, Sydney - 10.34am

TUESDAY
8th OCTOBER

morning

afternoon

WEDNESDAY
9th OCTOBER

morning

afternoon

MOON ENTERS CAPRICORN
Toronto - 5.38am, London - 10.38am,
Sydney - 8.38pm

THURSDAY
10th OCTOBER

morning

afternoon

1st QUARTER MOON
IN *Capricorn*
Toronto - 1.31pm, London - 6.31pm

**MARS IN CANCER
SQUARE CHIRON IN
ARIES**
Today through 16th October

FRIDAY
11th OCTOBER

morning

afternoon

1st QUARTER MOON
IN *Capricorn*
Sydney - 4.31am

**MOON ENTERS
AQUARIUS**
Toronto - 12.31pm, London - 5.31pm

SATURDAY
12th OCTOBER

morning

afternoon

**MOON ENTERS
AQUARIUS**

Sydney - 3.31am

SUNDAY
13th OCTOBER

morning

afternoon

**MOON ENTERS
PISCES**

Toronto - 3.55pm, London - 8.55pm

**MERCURY ENTERS
SCORPIO**

Toronto - 3.24pm, London - 8.24pm

MERCURY

IN *Scorpio*

Toronto, London 13 October - 3 November
Sydney 14 October - 4 November

THE MESSENGER

Mercury influences how we transmit and receive information, our ideas
and conversations as well as influencing movement, trade and travel.

Mercury strips off his diplomatic Libran suit and enters Scorpio. His focus
is singular and sharp. Beam like, it pierces through the depths and
illuminates what lives below, in the pitch blackness of oceanic trenches.

Not one for rash decisions, Mercury slows in Scorpio.
He savours each step of the journey as he delves into the mysteries of life.
Sex, death, fortunes made and scandal, loss and ruination
– he calls these home base.

His intensity can leave some folk queasy. They'll be captivated as his
attention is magnetic, and they'll learn a lot. He doesn't forget a thing,
and he is a brilliant orator and can weave a story replete with insanely lush,
juicy and salacious detail.

Mercury in Scorpios' curiosity extends beyond interpersonal relationships
and their complexities. He is a lover of the Grand Mysteries. The great
question of why are we all here? Where do we go after we die? How can we
pierce the veil of this reality to perceive the World of Spirit?

These lines of enquiry don't go down well with everyone. Same goes
for the conspiratorial bunnies he goes chasing down holes for. His very
nature can isolate him and separate him from the herd. Of course, their
plebeian attitudes bore him – but the ostracisation and his capacity
to read motivation make him suspicious and slow to trust.

You may find your intuition and perceptive capacities are heightened during this time. What mysteries are you going to tune into while Scorpio is in Mercury?

Brilliant memory – Fixated with facts
Emotionally intelligent – Unforgiving
Understanding – Salacious

I'VE BEEN THINKING ABOUT...
I JUST WANT TO SAY...

FULL MOON

Aries

PEAK ENERGY,
BLESSINGS & BLOSSOMS

17th October - Toronto 7.26pm,
London 12.26pm, Sydney 10.26am

Sun, Moon, Chiron, Mars and Pluto are still fixed in a cardinal grand cross – meaning that for a while we feel the spark and catch a glimpse of flaming Aries individualism . It's in check by considerable tension. We want to break free. We've got to break free... but that Libran Sun doesn't want the boat rocked. Mars in Cancer is clinging onto some very deep seated feelings (possibly anger and resentment) and Pluto in Capricorn is controlling the whole show. Complex.

Keep your head on... and your hard hat.

HOW HAVE INTENTIONS MADE
ON THE NEW MOON MANIFESTED?

_____

_____

_____

_____

_____

Transits

VENUS IN SCORPIO TRINE NEPTUNE IN PISCES

13th through 20th of October
Heightened Influence 15th through 17th October

A sweetness flows in through unexpected channels – a new dream may arrive no matter our age. Portents of a new direction alight with possibilities.

VENUS IN SCORPIO OPPOSITE URANUS IN TAURUS

11th through 19th October
Heightened Influence 13th through 16th October

Uranus is predictably unpredictable. Who knows what will happen once sparks fly and lightning erupts. Venus in Scorpio is ready for it. She lives for intensity. Are you open for a spell transformation?

MARS IN CANCER TRINE NEPTUNE IN PISCES

18th October through 8th November
Heightened Influence 25th October through 1st November

You may find that curious attraction and impulses pull you outside the orb of your usual routes. Is there rhythm or reason to what and who you desire? What is your longing pulling you towards?

Alternately a mist of fatigue may descend upon you and land you in bed – in which case, rest if you can. Take heart this isn't a permanent situation.

VENUS

IN *Sagittarius*

Toronto, London 18th October - 12th November
Sydney 18th October - 13th November

THE MUSE

Venus works in the sphere of love, desire, creativity and relationships. She influences our personal magnetism, tastes and resources.

LOVE AND DESIRE

The call of the wild and the open road – relationships that keep shifting and expanding and never grow old, stagnant or boring.

CREATIVITY AND INSPIRATION

Venus is inspired by the promise, the hunt and the fulfilment of learning. She looks to fill in the gaps of her experiences. If you are seeking to connect with her, follow the energy. Think horses galloping and the epic journey of migrating birds. Think whales singing their way around the globe and a life of travel that never ends.

THE MANNER OF RELATING

Venus is warm and gregarious, flighty and flirty. She may seem to be all in and then disappear in a heartbeat. Stagnancy is death to her. What you call comfortable and cosy she may call cloying and stifling. She needs room and trust and she'll give both of those to you. Just know that in her heart she is a wild boho nomad and resist the urge to try and pen her in.

Warm and gregarious – Irresponsible
Wild and free – Nowhere to be found
Exuberant – Exhausting

I'M SO INSPIRED BY... I LOVE...
IT DRIVES ME CRAZY WHEN...
EXPLORE WHEN THE MOOD STRIKES

The week ahead

M ....

T ....

W ....

T ....

F ....

S ....

S ....

The weekly transits

Mercury enters Scorpio
Venus in Scorpio trine
Neptune in Pisces
Venus in Scorpio opposite
Uranus in Taurus
Full Moon in Aries
Venus enters Sagittarius

MONDAY
14th OCTOBER

morning

afternoon

MOON ENTERS PISCES
Sydney - 6.55am

MERCURY ENTERS SCORPIO
Sydney - 6.24am

TUESDAY
15th OCTOBER

morning

afternoon

MOON ENTERS ARIES
Toronto - 4.34pm, London - 9.34pm

VENUS IN SCORPIO TRINE NEPTUNE IN PISCES
Today through 17th October

VENUS IN SCORPIO OPPOSITE URANUS IN TAURUS
Today through 21st June

WEDNESDAY
16th OCTOBER

morning

afternoon

MOON ENTERS ARIES
Sydney - 7.34am

THURSDAY
17th OCTOBER

morning

afternoon

FRIDAY
18th OCTOBER

morning

afternoon

FULL MOON IN *Aries*
Toronto - 7.26am, London - 12.26pm,
Sydney - 10.26pm

VENUS ENTERS SAGITTARIUS
Toronto - 4.28pm, London - 9..28pm,
Sydney - 6.28am

SATURDAY
19th OCTOBER

morning

afternoon

SUNDAY
20th OCTOBER

morning

afternoon

MOON ENTERS
GEMINI
Toronto - 5.43pm, London - 10.43pm,
Sydney - 8.43am

SUN IN SCORPIO

Transmuting Poison into Medicine

THE EIGHTH HOUSE - FIXED WATER
PLANETARY RULER - MARS & PLUTO

Toronto, London 22nd October - 21st November
Sydney 23rd October - 22nd November

Taking leave of the lovely, fair and broadminded Libra, the Sun enters the deeply personal and private realm of Scorpio.

Scorpio's sting is legendary. You'll never forget it. They never forget – Anything. Perhaps it's because they feel things to the core... as in, to the very heart of their being. Words and actions that may bounce off others, pierce them. Don't mistake this for weakness. Remember, Mars rules this watery realm and he functions in a particular way here.

Scorpio desires the sting. Without it, how would he learn? Through his profound, intuitive capacity, he becomes the poison and transmutes it. Alchemising it into medicine, it can be a bitter draught to receive.
If you are the beneficiary of the Scorpio's sting, before you lash out at the injustice of it, take a deep and introspective look. What did you do to deserve it? That action you took ten years ago – you thought it was all fine because it'd been talked through and forgiven? Hmm. Scorpio remembers. His form of justice doesn't require many words.

The capacity to wait for the perfect alignment of circumstance and consciousness is an art form. Scorpio will deliver his well-considered words or actions at the precise moment of maximum impact. His justice is served when genuine awareness of the effect of the initial injury is experienced by the transgressor. Possibly all the consequences that have followed as well. This sounds like a lot to carry, but Scorpio is backed by Mars AND Pluto. They are connected to a profound power source.

However his sting isn't the whole picture. You will find Scorpio to be incredibly understanding, loyal and loving. Compassion runs deep, for they understand many of the motivations that we hide from ourselves and love us for being the humble, fallible humans that we are.

Those with a strong Scorpio influence in their natal charts are spiritually-minded, imaginative and creative beings. When we are generous with our warmth and understanding they glow luminescently and will share their keen insights and some of their secrets with us.

Scorpio season
CONSIDERATIONS

Am I holding onto anger caused by old wounds?
If so, how might I address this?
How is my mediative or spiritual discipline?
I would like to harness the Scorpio energy by...

....

....

....

3rd QUARTER MOON

Aries

REFLECT & RELEASE

10th October - Toronto 4.03am,
London 9.03am, Sydney 4.31pm

Once more, we are asked to let go of what is no longer serving us. In this case, it's the serious dross of life that is weighing us down. The Leonine Moon is asking us to stretch it out and limber up for some fun. Games night? Date night? Dinner party? Something gloriously relaxed and easy to put together. Mars and Pluto are sitting at the edge grumbling about something, just let 'em. Throw them a smile in the way you might your favourite grumchkin.

WHAT ARE YOU ASKED TO PUSH THROUGH
AND WHAT DO YOU NEED TO RELEASE
BEFORE NEXT WEEK'S NEW MOON?

Transits

SUN IN LIBRA (THEN INTO SCORPIO) SQUARE PLUTO IN CAPRICORN

20th through 28th of October
Heightened Influence 22nd through 24th October

Know you've got it in you to pass these trials. Hold your ground if need be, but be prepared to let go of outmoded strategies and to change tactics if needed. New terrain is being encountered.

MARS IN CANCER OPPOSITE PLUTO IN CAPRICORN

21st October through 19th November
Heightened Influence 30th October through 7th November

Hands on swords, eyes locked, both parties are waiting for the slightest twitch to swing into motion.

You have options: there's full on confrontation, or looking away – or you could de-arm, walk away, and wait for a less emotionally-loaded time to have a conversation.

This transit can also portend a time of a massive breakthrough; however it plays out, it will alter the landscape.

VENUS IN SAGITTARIUS SQUARE SATURN IN PISCES

25th October through 2nd November
Heightened Influence 28th through 30th October

Venus rules our relationships and finances and, if you are currently uncertain about either, now's the time to step back and reflect on how you wish to proceed. If there are important decisions to be made, do you have all the information yet? Or are you waiting on another person's move?

The week ahead

M

T

W

T

F

S

S

The weekly transits

Mars in Cancer trine Neptune in Pisces
Sun in Libra (and then into Scorpio)
square Pluto in Capricorn
Sun enters Scorpio
Mars in Cancer opposite
Pluto in Capricorn
Venus in Sagittarius square
Saturn in Pisces
Third Quarter Moon in Leo

MONDAY
21st OCTOBER

morning

afternoon

MOON ENTERS CANCER
Toronto - 7.50pm

TUESDAY
22nd OCTOBER

morning

afternoon

MOON ENTERS CANCER
London - 12.50am, Sydney - 9.50am

SUN ENTERS SCORPIO
Toronto - 6.15 pm, London - 11.15 pm

SUN IN LIBRA (AND THEN INTO SCORPIO) SQUARE PLUTO IN CAPRICORN
Today through 24th October

WEDNESDAY
23rd OCTOBER

morning

afternoon

SUN ENTERS SCORPIO
Sydney - 9.15 am

THURSDAY
24th OCTOBER

morning

afternoon

FRIDAY
25th OCTOBER

morning

afternoon

3rd QUARTER MOON

IN *Leo*

Toronto - 4.03 am, London - 9.03 am,
Sydney - 7.03 pm

**MARS IN CANCER
TRINE NEPTUNE IN
PISCES**

Today through 1st November

SATURDAY
26th OCTOBER

morning

afternoon

SUNDAY
27th OCTOBER

morning

afternoon

MOON ENTERS VIRGO
Toronto - 11.47pm , London - 4.47pm

NEW MOON

Scorpio

PLANTING SEEDS

1st November - Toronto 8.46am,
London 12.46pm, Sydney 11.46pm

There is a particular flavour of intensity to the Scorpio Moon. Tonight's New Moon is rich with potential. Mars and Pluto, the two rulers of Scorpio, are locked in, staring one another down from opposite sides of the heavens. Full standoff position. Meanwhile, Mercury, still in Scorpio and equipped to deal with complexity, has opened communication with Neptune and Uranus – powerful allies who will help shift the focus. Uranus, through surprise and awe, and Neptune by dissolving and dazzling.

The incoming communication may be highly inspirational – be it through conversation, daydreaming or meditation.
What a day... a night! Be open to new information as you make your intentions as there's a lot of moving parts at play.

New Moon in Scorpio themes: Emotional honesty and integrity. Courage to face the truth. Surprising and possibly highly-inspiring communication.

NEW MOON INTENTIONS

....

....

....

Transits

MERCURY IN SCORPIO OPPOSITE URANUS IN TAURUS

28th October through 3rd November
Heightened Influence 30th October through 1st November

Pay attention to the subtle currents during this period if you've been waiting for information or news. The penny may drop. It's not what you think.

VENUS IN SAGITTARIUS OPPOSITE JUPITER IN GEMINI

31st October through 7th November
Heightened Influence 3rd through 5th November

It's a big love. Massive. Huge. Ginormous.
Is it too big to last?
Was it all just hot air?

MERCURY

IN *Sagittarius*

Toronto, London 2nd November - 8th January
Sydney 3rd November - 8th January

THE MESSENGER

Mercury influences how we transmit and receive information, our ideas and conversations as well as influencing movement, trade and travel.

Mercury in Sagittarius has a hunger for knowledge and his expansive mind can glean it in multiple ways. As the student of life he can hear news on the winds that others would miss, and off he shoots – chasing the experience to fill in the blank spaces of his experience.

Doing the thing isn't the same as reading about it after all. Reading is great too, as are podcasts, conversations with strangers on public transport, digital and arcane libraries and also forests. Nothing is off limits. He wants to know everything.

You may find him chatting with an AI or trying to see if bots get jokes. For Mercury in Sagittarius the pursuit of knowledge is sacred duty, but that doesn't make it dour and grey. He brings life and warmth to cold thoughts and serious matters.

Mercury in Sagittarius knows that crazy has wisdom to it and that the heart has an intelligence that differs from the knowledge of the head and he'll seek a system to link the two – or the three... the gut has its own language and intuition too. You see, there is no end to what can be learnt, and experienced.

A brilliant time for studying, being a 'student of life', expanding your mind through philosophy and sharing your experiences through teaching.

Eternally enthusiastic – Runs out of steam
Can turn anything into a story – Forgets the facts
Speaks from experience – Self importance

I'VE BEEN THINKING ABOUT...
I JUST WANT TO SAY...

The week ahead

M

T

W

T

F

S

S

The weekly transits

Mercury in Scorpio opposite
Uranus in Taurus
Venus in Sagittarius opposite
Jupiter in Gemini
New Moon in Scorpio
Mercury enters Sagittarius

morning

afternoon

MOON ENTERS VIRGO
Sydney - 2.47am

MERCURY IN SCORPIO OPPOSITE URANUS IN TAURUS
Today through 1st November

VENUS IN SAGITTARIUS SQUARE SATURN IN PISCES
Today through 30th October

TUESDAY
29th OCTOBER

morning

afternoon

WEDNESDAY
30th OCTOBER

morning

afternoon

MOON ENTERS LIBRA
Toronto - 12.30am, London - 4.30am, Sydney - 3.30pm

MARS IN CANCER OPPOSITE PLUTO IN CAPRICORN
Today through 7th November

VENUS IN SAGITTARIUS OPPOSITE JUPITER IN GEMINI
Today through 5th November

morning

morning

afternoon

afternoon

NEW MOON IN
Scorpio
Toronto - 8.46am, London - 12.46pm,
Sydney - 11.46pm

SATURDAY
2nd NOVEMBER

morning

afternoon

**MERCURY ENTERS
SAGITTARIUS**
Toronto - 3.18pm, London - 7.18pm

SUNDAY
3rd NOVEMBER

morning

afternoon

**MERCURY ENTERS
SAGITTARIUS**
Sydney - 6.18am

**MOON ENTERS
SAGITTARIUS**
Toronto - 1.19am, London - 5.19am,
Sydney - 4.19pm

MARS ENTERS LEO
Toronto - 12.10pm, London - 4.10am

MARS

IN *Leo*

Toronto, London, Sydney 4th November

MARS TURNS RETROGRADE IN LEO
Toronto, London 6th December, Sydney 7th December

MARS RETROGRADE RE-ENTERS CANCER
Toronto, London, Sydney 6th January

THE WARRIOR

Mars works through our drives and desires; our ambitions and how we achieve them. He sets and secures our personal boundaries and defends us against those who transgress them.

DRIVES AND DESIRES

Stretching out from his epically long stay in Cancer, Mars catches fire and so do we... momentarily. He will be returning to Cancer to readdress some inner issues before confidently moving forwards. But for now he has a rollicking good time as Leo reignites his high-drive and work ethic. Work becomes like play and we are driven to perform our tasks with enthusiasm and pride.

AMBITION AND WORK

Mars loves to work. Especially if it serves his pride and community. He's generous with his time and knowledge, making him a natural leader. But, he needs to be appreciated. It'll all grind to a halt if the effort he lovingly expends gets met with silence or criticism.

BOUNDARIES AND PROTECTION

Mars in Leo has the roar you'd imagine. You'll know all about it if you've crossed a boundary. So too will any would-be fool who tries to have a go at his loved ones. It doesn't take much to get an angry horde together with his charismatic influence and leadership qualities.

When Mars is in Taurus you may experience: Enthusiasm, love of work, sports and physical activities, pride in accomplishments.

Difficulties you may encounter: Inflexibility, selfishness, a look-at-me attitude and a need for all the spotlight.

INTENTIONS, INSIGHTS AND REFLECTIONS

1st QUARTER MOON

Aquarius

MOMENTUM & GROWTH

9th December - Toronto 12.54am,
London 5.54am, Sydney 4.54pm

The unique and curious insights of this Aquarian Moon are amplified by an
easy-going trine from Jupiter in Gemini. There is much to process right now!
If you have any mental blockages at this time, reach out and ask for answers.
These may come through mediation, conversation or wherever
you harness your information.
If you are free flowing at the moment – listen closely,
inspiration and insight may be incoming.

WHAT ACTIONS AM I TAKING TO FULFIL
INTENTIONS SET ON THE NEW MOON?

The week ahead

M

T

W

T

F

S

S

The weekly transits

Mars enters Leo
First Quarter Moon in Aquarius

morning

afternoon

MARS ENTERS LEO
Sydney - 3.10pm

TUESDAY
5th NOVEMBER

morning

afternoon

WEDNESDAY
6th NOVEMBER

morning

afternoon

**MOON ENTERS
CAPRICORN**

Toronto - 10.17am, London - 3.17pm

**MOON ENTERS
CAPRICORN**

Sydney - 2.17am

THURSDAY
7th NOVEMBER

morning

afternoon

MOON ENTERS AQUARIUS
Toronto - 5.48pm, London - 10.48pm

FRIDAY
8th NOVEMBER

morning

afternoon

MOON ENTERS AQUARIUS
Sydney - 9.48am

SATURDAY
9th NOVEMBER

morning

afternoon

1st QUARTER MOON IN

Aquarius

Toronto - 12.54am, London - 5.54am,
Sydney - 4.54pm

MOON ENTERS PISCES
Toronto - 11.00am

SUNDAY
10th NOVEMBER

morning

afternoon

**MOON ENTERS
PISCES**
London - 4.00am, Sydney - 3.00pm

Transits

MERCURY IN SAGITTARIUS OPPOSITE JUPITER IN GEMINI

Part 1

13th through 26th November
Heightened Influence 17th through 20th November
This transit comes in three parts.

Mercury in Sagittarius transmutes his experience into wisdom and devours philosophy. Living religious traditions, and how they compare across cultures, is of special interest to him as it combines both philosophy and his personal experience.

Jupiter, as we have been discovering, makes everything BIGGER. In Gemini it's as if they have just snipped the ribbon and now the superhighway of information is flowing – thick and fast towards us. Possibly running us over. It's a lot for humans to process.

When these two stand in opposition there is A LOT to consider and to talk about. Are brain implants really the way of the future? What does it mean if a human being is hooked up to the internet? Do you believe it's necessary to have a chip implant to pay for groceries? (Isn't that the mark of the beast that John saw, from his island cave all those two thousand odd years ago?)

Don't shy from the conversation. Yes, some voices are definitely louder than others, but we all have a right to voice our opinions.

SUN IN SCORPIO OPPOSITE URANUS IN TAURUS

12th through 21st of November
Heightened Influence 16th through 19th November

The Scorpio Sun isn't all seriousness and as it approaches Uranus in Taurus the mood begins to shift. Some may feel this as a delightful break in the tedium and have a minor rebellion against their schedules. For others the impulse to rebel strikes deeper – bringing up a deep frustration at the old paradigms and patterns that habitually dictate their lives. Either way, it's a song of the sun to remind you that you are at your very essence, a free human being.

VENUS IN CAPRICORN SQUARE NORTH NODE IN ARIES AND SOUTH NODE IN LIBRA

12th November 20th November
Heightened Influence 15th through 18th November

We have a choice to make. In this perfect moment poised between the nostalgia of the past and dreams projected on the future. Take heart, be brave – your courage will find you. The future seems daunting but new doors are always opening as we walk towards it – revealing just what we need for life's next phase.

FULL MOON
Taurus

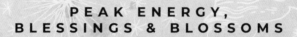

PEAK ENERGY,
BLESSINGS & BLOSSOMS

15th November - Toronto 4.27pm, London 9.27pm
16th November - Sydney 8.27am

Grounded yet zappy and ecstatic, this Taurean Full Moon offers up a lush, sensual and surprising bounty. It's seriously delightful and much needed. The emotional intensity of the Scorpio Sun meets the warm folds of Taurean arms. We all need the sweetness of touch and shared warmth. An evening for a party of a hundred or the intimate delicacy of two. Who are you sharing tonight with?

HOW HAVE INTENTIONS MADE ON THE NEW MOON MANIFESTED?

....

....

....

....

....

....

VENUS

IN *Capricorn*

Toronto, London 12th November - 7th December
Sydney 13th November - 7th December

Venus enters Capricorn for the second time in the course of this astrological cycle. Her first visit was on the 23rd January, which you can find in the first week of this Diary. This gives you a wonderful opportunity to review your experiences last Venus in Capricorn time and to see if you can detect her elegant influence as she moves through Capricorn again.

HOW DID I DETECT AND EXPERIENCE VENUS'S PASSAGE THROUGH CAPRICORN EARLIER ON IN THE YEAR? ARE THERE ANY REPEATING THEMES?

The week ahead

M

T

W

T

F

S

S

The weekly transits

Venus enters Capricorn
Full Moon in Taurus
Mercury in Sagittarius opposite
Jupiter in Gemini (Part 1)

morning

afternoon

TUESDAY
12th NOVEMBER

morning

afternoon

MOON ENTERS ARIES
Toronto - 1.26am, London - 6.26am,
Sydney - 5.26pm

**VENUS ENTERS
CAPRICORN**
Toronto - 1.26pm, London - 6.26pm

WEDNESDAY
13th NOVEMBER

morning

afternoon

**VENUS ENTERS
CAPRICORN**
Sydney - 5.26am

THURSDAY
14th NOVEMBER

morning

afternoon

FRIDAY
15th NOVEMBER

morning

afternoon

FULL MOON IN

Taurus

Toronto - 4.27pm, London - 9.27pm

VENUS IN CAPRICORN SQUARE NORTH NODE IN ARIES AND SOUTH NODE IN LIBRA

Today through 18th November

MOON ENTERS TAURUS

Toronto - 1.59am, London - 6.59am, Sydney - 5.59pm

SATURDAY
16th NOVEMBER

morning

afternoon

FULL MOON IN *Taurus*
Sydney - 8.27am

SUN IN SCORPIO OPPOSITE URANUS IN TAURUS
Today through 19th November

MOON ENTERS GEMINI
Toronto - 2.09am, London - 7.09am

MOON ENTERS GEMINI
Sydney - 6.09pm

SUNDAY
17th NOVEMBER

morning

afternoon

MOON ENTERS CANCER
Toronto - 3.50am, London - 8.50am

MERCURY IN SAGITTARIUS OPPOSITE JUPITER IN GEMINI (PART 1)
Today through 20th November

3rd QUARTER MOON

Virgo

REFLECT & RELEASE

22nd November - Toronto 8.27pm
23rd November - London 1.27am, Sydney 12.27pm

It's that time again – what have you learnt this Moon Cycle and what needs to be let go of and released? The Virgo Moon is right at home here – utilise her organisational brilliance to make a list. How about keep and chuck piles, plus a maybe pile for the things you are not quite sure about? It's an inspired day/night to clean up house. Physically and mentally.

WHAT ARE YOU ASKED TO PUSH THROUGH
AND WHAT DO YOU NEED TO RELEASE
AS WE HEAD INTO NEXT WEEK'S NEW MOON?

The week ahead

M

T

W

T

F

S

S

The weekly transits

Pluto re enters Aquarius
Sun enters Sagittarius
Third Quarter Moon in Virgo

morning

afternoon

**MOON ENTERS
CANCER**
Sydney - 7.50pm

TUESDAY
19th NOVEMBER

morning

afternoon

WEDNESDAY
20th NOVEMBER

morning

afternoon

MOON ENTERS LEO
Toronto - 8.51am

PLUTO RE-ENTERS AQUARIUS

THURSDAY
21st NOVEMBER

morning

afternoon

MOON ENTERS LEO
London - 1.51pm, Sydney - 12.51am

**SUN ENTERS
SAGITTARIUS**
Toronto - 2.56pm, London - 7.56pm

FRIDAY
22nd NOVEMBER

morning

afternoon

**SUN ENTERS
SAGITTARIUS**
Sydney - 6.56am

3rd QUARTER MOON
IN *Virgo*
Toronto - 8.27pm

SATURDAY
23rd NOVEMBER

morning

afternoon

SUNDAY
24th NOVEMBER

morning

afternoon

3rd QUARTER MOON
IN *Virgo*
London - 1.27am, Sydney - 12.27pm

SUN IN SAGITTARIUS
The Great Adventure

THE NINTH HOUSE - MUTABLE FIRE
PLANETARY RULER - JUPITER

Toronto, London 21st November - 21st December
Sydney 22nd November - 21st December

The Sun leaves the watery depths of Scorpio and shines enthusiastically through the stars of Sagittarius.

There's not much that can stop the indomitable spirit of the Sagittarian Sun. Don't think for a minute that the pain and suffering of life has been less bleak or brutal for those born under his auspices. They just find a way to weave it into a legend. A story that becomes, with each retelling, ever more akin to an archetypal myth. They're not, however, greedy for the limelight. They'll help you understand your destiny with the same amount of pathos and passion – if the Stars align and the timing is right.

There's a natural confidence at work here and we can detect Jupiter's touch. A liferaft keeps them afloat, feet tucked away, safe from sharks with only an old palm frond for a paddle. Deep feelings can be skated over as they row into shore – eager for the next grand adventure to begin.
They're not blind to the depths, and they are profoundly respectful of the mysteries that lie below the surface, but feelings can get a person lodged in and they're suspicious of any type of entrapment.
They prefer the *breadth* of things.

Big understandings. Big ideas. The sort that makes sense of why we are all on the planet to begin with. Sagittarius inspires us to soar to the inner workings of how our universe was created and what our purpose is here on Earth. The Sagittarian element inspires us to weave our way through secular, materialistic, spiritual and religious viewpoints. Sagittarians understand that no singular doctrine, belief system or entity holds the full picture.

There is a glorious optimism that propels them ever forwards, certain that the ultimate truth is out there to be found.

Sagittarius season

CONSIDERATIONS

*Am I moving enough? Running, walking, swimming
– all movement will help connect you with the Sagittarian impulse.
What are the big ideas that fascinate and inspire me?
Any travel or study plans? A research trip perhaps?
I would like to harness the Sagittarian gifts by...*

MERCURY RETROGRADE
in *Sagittarius*

London and Toronto: Mercury Retrograde in Sagittarius - 26th November, Mercury Stations - 13th December, Mercury turns Direct - 18th December
Sydney: Mercury Retrograde in Sagittarius - 25th November, Mercury Stations - 13th December, Mercury turns Direct - 19th December

Ah! Here we are again. The Cosmos has granted us a reprieve from the push ever forwards as Mercury spends the next three weeks retracing his steps. What do you need to recover? What needs extra checking and processing? It's time to retrieve that certain thing that's been forgotten. You'll know what it is when you see it.

Mercury Retro rules apply – it's best to avoid signing contracts, releasing projects and anything else where easy, clean momentum is desired. If you have something important already scheduled, go with it, and treat any hiccups as the humorous side to Mercury retro... If you can! Be mindful of phones and computers. Cracked screens and wet phones can sure hold things up.

INSIGHTS OVER THE COURSE OF THIS MERCURY RETROGRADE IN SAGITTARIUS...

CONTEMPLATIONS

NEW MOON
Sagittarius

PLANTING SEEDS

1st December - Toronto 1.20am,
London 6.20am, Sydney 5.20pm

In the star-filled sky, the Sun and Moon meet and it's time to dream of your intentions. Dream big and true tonight. Summon forth your adventurous spirit and see where she wants to take you. What inspires you the most? When and where are you your happiest? What circumstances facilitate the flowing of your inherent wisdom? Follow the breadcrumbs. Your life is your grand adventure – where is it taking you and where do you want to go?

New Moon in Sagittarius themes: Optimism, adventure, travel and the pursuit of truth.

NEW MOON INTENTIONS

....

....

....

....

....

....

....

Transits

SUN IN SAGITTARIUS TRINE MARS IN LEO

22nd November through 3rd December
Heightened Influence 25th through 29th November

Mars over in Leo is sending forth his passion, power and enthusiasm to the already activated Sagittarian Sun. Welcome in the extra energy and ride the busy, productive and, at times, jubilant waves. You'll achieve a lot with very little effort or strain.

The week ahead

M

T

W

T

F

S

S

The weekly transits

Sun in Sagittarius trine Mars in Aries
Mercury turns Retrograde in Sagittarius
New Moon in Sagittarius

MONDAY
25th NOVEMBER

morning

afternoon

MOON ENTERS LIBRA
Toronto - 6.20am, London - 11.20am,
Sydney - 10.20pm

SUN IN SAGITTARIUS TRINE MARS IN LEO
Today through 29th November

MERCURY TURNS RETROGRADE IN SAGITTARIUS
Toronto - 9.42pm

TUESDAY
26th NOVEMBER

morning

afternoon

WEDNESDAY
27th NOVEMBER

morning

afternoon

MERCURY TURNS RETROGRADE IN SAGITTARIUS

London - 2.42am, Sydney - 1.42pm

THURSDAY
28th NOVEMBER

morning

afternoon

FRIDAY
29th NOVEMBER

morning

afternoon

MOON ENTERS
SCORPIO
Toronto - 7.21pm, London - 12.21am,
Sydney - 11.21am

SATURDAY
30th NOVEMBER

morning

afternoon

SUNDAY
1st DECEMBER

morning

afternoon

**MOON ENTERS
SAGITTARIUS**
Toronto - 6.31am, London - 11.31am,
Sydney - 10.31pm

NEW MOON IN
Sagittarius
Toronto - 1.20am, London - 6.20am,
Sydney - 5.20pm

Transits

MERCURY RETROGRADE IN SAGITTARIUS OPPOSITE JUPITER IN GEMINI

Part 2

2nd through 9th December
Heightened Influence 3rd through 6th December

The conversation has been reviewed, new data has come in, and opinions have been voiced. A proper assessment needs to be made before moving forwards.

You may find yourself as part of a collective discussion – or this transit could be affecting you on a more intimate level. If so, take a deep breath and follow the memories and piece the puzzle together in the order that information arrives. Answers will be coming soon.

VENUS IN CAPRICORN (AND THEN INTO AQUARIUS) CONJUNCT PLUTO IN AQUARIUS

3rd through 12th December
Heightened Influence 6th through 9th December

Venus in Capricorn likes to conserve, and she inspires an infrastructure that can contain a lasting legacy. When meeting Pluto she can become obsessed with attaining her desires, wants, and highly-specific needs. She can mistake these for love and this leads to curious entanglements. She would do anything for love... but would she do THAT?

Keep an eye open to check if attentiveness has turned to infatuation... inching ever closer to becoming toxic. Spoiler: Venus escapes. Freedom and honesty are high on the Venus-in-Aquarius' checklist of desirable qualities.

SUN IN SAGITTARIUS OPPOSITE JUPITER IN GEMINI

3rd through 13th December
Heightened Influence 6th through 9th December

You know that moment when it all makes sense? That wonderful instance when you see that all those detours and byways life has taken you down have led you to here, right now. There's not one square inch of your past that you wouldn't claim.
That wisdom, learnt and hard-earned, is now a part of who you are, and there's no doubt that you're wiser for it.

Utilise the knowledge gleaned from past experiences to move forwards with confidence and optimism.

_____

_____

_____

_____

_____

_____

_____

_____

VENUS

in *Aquarius*

Toronto, London Sydney 7th December - 3rd January

Venus enters Aquarius for the second time in the astrological cycle covered in this Diary. Her first visit began on the 16th February, which you can find in the last week of the Aquarius Season. We just experienced our second Capricorn Venus, and now we get to experiment with Venus in Aquarius. Have you detected traces of her influence? Can you find the theme? This is Venus at her most broad minded and freedom loving.

HOW DID I DETECT AND EXPERIENCE THE VENUS PASSAGE THROUGH AQUARIUS EARLIER THIS YEAR? CAN YOU FIND A THEME?

MARS RETROGRADE

IN *Leo*

Toronto, London 7th December
Sydney 8th December

The Warrior is spent. Mars needs rest. Previously he had a long stay in Cancer – and now he wants to make his way back to the emotional intensity of that realm.
What happened to make him so heartfelt and homesick? It's the need for safety and nurturing that calls him. We all need a break and we all need a Mother's love. She who smoothes our worries and knows the parts of us that we were too young to recall.

Mars re-enters Cancer in early December but until then he is retracing his steps through Leo.

WHAT UNFINISHED BUSINESS IS MARS LEADING ME TOWARDS? IT MAY NEED TIME TO REVEAL ITSELF – IT'S A SLOW MARCH BACK.

The week ahead

M

T

W

T

F

S

S

The weekly transits

Mercury Retrograde in Sagittarius
opposite Jupiter in Gemini (Part 2)
Venus in Capricorn (then into Aquarius)
conjunct Pluto in Aquarius
Sun in Sagittarius opposite
Jupiter in Gemini
Venus enters Aquarius
Mars goes Retrograde in Leo

MONDAY
2nd DECEMBER

morning

afternoon

MOON ENTERS CAPRICORN
Toronto - 4.09pm, London - 9.09pm

morning

morning

afternoon

afternoon

MOON ENTERS
CAPRICORN
Sydney - 8.09am

MERCURY
RETROGRADE
IN SAGITTARIUS
OPPOSITE JUPITER
IN GEMINI (PART 2)
Today through 6th December

MOON ENTERS
AQUARIUS
Toronto - 11.21pm

morning

morning

afternoon

afternoon

MARS GOES RETROGRADE IN LEO
Toronto - 6.33pm, London - 11.33pm

VENUS IN CAPRICORN (THEN INTO AQUARIUS) CONJUNCT PLUTO IN AQUARIUS
Today through 9th December

MOON ENTERS AQUARIUS
London - 4.21am, Sydney - 3.21pm

SUN IN SAGITTARIUS OPPOSITE JUPITER IN GEMINI
Today through 20th December

morning

morning

afternoon

afternoon

MOON ENTERS PISCES
Toronto - 4.49am, London - 9.49am,
Sydney - 8.49pm

VENUS ENTERS AQUARIUS
Toronto - 1.13am, London - 6.13am,
Sydney - 5.13pm

MARS GOES RETROGRADE IN LEO
Sydney - 10.33am

1st QUARTER MOON
IN *Pisces*
Toronto - 10.26am, London - 3.26pm

1st QUARTER MOON

Pisces

MOMENTUM & GROWTH

8th December - Toronto 10.26am, London 3.26pm
9th December - Sydney 2.26am

With both Mercury and Mars retrograde it may feel like you are slipping backwards into some life-sucking loop.

The Pisces Moon says 'Don't fight it - life is hard enough.' She just swiped by Saturn a few hours ago, so she knows. It'll pass. Re-evaluate your intentions – if you've got the energy – and hand the rest of it back over to the cosmos.

HOW ARE THOSE INTENTIONS GROWING?

Transits

SUN IN SAGITTARIUS TRINE
CHIRON IN ARIES

6th through 16th December
Heightened Influence 9th through 13th December

Take a moment and imagine feeling full of enthusiasm and vital life force. Now, invite in the healing impulses available at this time. Recharge and rid yourself of any grey malaise that may have snuck into your energetic field. Allow the muck to drain away, carrying with it old stories of wounding – especially those slights and insults that made you doubt your individual shine and playful capacity to create the life you want.

MERCURY STATIONS DIRECT IN SAGITTARIUS
TRINE MARS RETROGRADE IN LEO

13th through 19th December
Heightened Influence 13th through 9th December

Conversations turn towards moving ahead and plans for the future – but it may not be the time to action them just yet. Mars, and the impact that he has on our vital forces, continues to retrace his steps through Leo, then he turns introspective as he edges closer to Cancer. Doesn't mean your plans for the future are not going to happen! Maybe, just not yet.

MERCURY DIRECT IN SAGITTARIUS
OPPOSITE JUPITER IN GEMINI
Part 3

23rd December through 8th January
Heightened Influence 26th through 31st December

There is a consequence to all things. Thoughts have been distilled and the over-the-top and inflated ideas have been discarded and forgotten. We're at the serious end of business now and we're ready.

With the Sun entering Capricorn we have come full cycle. Thank you so much for travelling alongside us... Wishing you all the very best for the holiday season and New Year. Ariel x

FULL MOON
Gemini
CONJUNCT JUPITER

PEAK ENERGY,
BLESSINGS & BLOSSOMS

15th December - Toronto 4.00am,
London 9.00am, Sydney 8.00pm

This Full Moon has Jupiter amplifying EVERYTHING. It's big – like a massive party, festive-season big! Keep an ear open for conversations with long lost lovers, friends or family. (Remember Mercury and Mars are still retrograde.) Saturn is holding court, adding an earnest, responsible designated-driver vibe – but otherwise, it's sparkly. Glitter-and-streamers sparkly.

HOW HAVE INTENTIONS MADE
ON THE NEW MOON MANIFESTED?

MUSINGS

The week ahead

M

T

W

T

F

S

S

The weekly transits

Sun in Sagittarius trine Chiron in Aries
First Quarter Moon in Pisces
Full Moon in Gemini

MONDAY
9th DECEMBER

morning

afternoon

1st QUARTER MOON
in *Pisces*
Sydney - 2.26am

SUN IN SAGITTARIUS TRINE CHIRON IN ARIES
Today through 13th December

MOON ENTERS ARIES
Toronto - 8.38am, London - 1.38pm

TUESDAY
10th DECEMBER

morning

afternoon

WEDNESDAY
11th DECEMBER

morning

afternoon

MOON ENTERS ARIES
Sydney - 12.38am

THURSDAY
12th DECEMBER

morning

afternoon

**MOON ENTERS
TAURUS**
Toronto - 10.55am, London - 3.55pm

**MOON ENTERS
TAURUS**
Sydney - 2.55am

FRIDAY
13th DECEMBER

morning

afternoon

**MOON ENTERS
GEMINI**
Toronto - 12.22pm, London - 5.22pm

**MERCURY STATIONS
DIRECT IN
SAGITTARIUS TRINE
MARS RETROGRADE
IN LEO**
Today through 9th December

SATURDAY
14th DECEMBER

morning

afternoon

SUNDAY
15th DECEMBER

morning

afternoon

FULL MOON IN

Gemini

Toronto - 4.00am, London - 9.00am,
Sydney - 8.00pm

MOON ENTERS
GEMINI

Sydney - 4.22am

MOON ENTERS
CANCER

Toronto - 2.21pm, London - 7.21pm

The week ahead

M ....

T ....

W ....

T ....

F ....

S ....

S ....

The weekly transits

The Sun enters Capricorn
Third Quarter Moon in Libra

morning

....
....
....
....
....

afternoon

....
....
....
....
....
....

**MOON ENTERS
CANCER**
Sydney - 6.21am

TUESDAY
17th DECEMBER

morning

afternoon

WEDNESDAY
18th DECEMBER

morning

afternoon

MOON ENTERS LEO
Toronto - 6.39pm, London - 11.39pm

MOON ENTERS LEO
Sydney - 10.39am

THURSDAY
19th DECEMBER

morning

afternoon

FRIDAY
20th DECEMBER

morning

afternoon

**MOON ENTERS
VIRGO**

Toronto - 2.37am, London - 7.37am,
Sydney - 6.37pm

SATURDAY
21st DECEMBER

morning

afternoon

SUNDAY
22nd DECEMBER

morning

afternoon

SUN ENTERS
CAPRICORN
Toronto - 4.21am, London - 9.21am,
Sydney - 8.21pm

3rd QUARTER MOON
IN *Libra*
Toronto - 5.18pm, London - 10.18pm

The week ahead

M
....
....

T
....
....

W
....
....

T
....
....

F
....
....

S
....
....

S
....
....

MONDAY
23rd DECEMBER

morning
....
....
....
....
....

afternoon
....
....
....
....
....
....

The weekly transits

Mercury Direct in Sagittarius
opposite Jupiter in Gemini (Part 3)

3rd QUARTER MOON

IN *Libra*

Sydney - 9.18am

TUESDAY
24th DECEMBER

morning

afternoon

WEDNESDAY
25th DECEMBER

morning

afternoon

MOON ENTERS
SCORPIO
Toronto - 3.07am, London - 8.07am,
Sydney - 7.07pm

THURSDAY
26th DECEMBER

morning

afternoon

**MERCURY DIRECT
IN SAGITTARIUS
OPPOSITE JUPITER
IN GEMINI (PART 3)**
Today through 31st December

FRIDAY
27th DECEMBER

morning

afternoon

**MOON ENTERS
SAGITTARIUS**
Toronto - 2.47pm, London - 7.47pm

SATURDAY
28th DECEMBER

morning

afternoon

SUNDAY
29th DECEMBER

morning

afternoon

MOON ENTERS
SAGITTARIUS
Sydney - 6.47am

The week ahead

M

T

W

T

F

S

S

morning

afternoon

The weekly transits

New Moon in Capricorn

TUESDAY
31st DECEMBER

morning

afternoon

WEDNESDAY
1st JANUARY

morning

afternoon

Thank You Team!

Thank you Melanie Spears for your faith in the process and the project. It's a GRAND adventure and I appreciate your enthusiasm, inspiration and can-do ANYTHING attitude.
givingthanks.co

Thank you Stephanie Jones for bringing your refined aesthetic sense, knowledge of fonts, spacing and all things balance. Your fastidious attention to detail is a never-ending source of amazement to me.
@sleepyhollowcreative

Thank you Melissa Williams for breathing your magic across the front cover and background pages. I deeply respect your special light-filled wisps and deep understanding of aesthetics.
Misprint.com.au

Editors deluxe! Thank you to Lee Buchanan and Alan Mills for your patience and precision, your word play and dramatic exactitude! I breathe easier knowing that your fine minds have scanned for, and corrected errors.

First published in Australia in 2023 by Melanie Spears for Giving Thanks.

PO Box 31 Ocean Shores NSW Australia 2483

© Ariel Korobacz 2023

Printed in China on wood free paper.

ISBN 978-0-645391015